McWILLIAMS

Product Development

The *Electronic Business* Series

Product Development: Success Through Product And Cycle-time Excellence

Michael E. McGrath

Michael T. Anthony

Amram R. Shapiro

Butterworth–Heinemann
Boston London Oxford Singapore Sydney Toronto Wellington

We dedicate this book to the clients of Pittiglio Rabin Todd
& McGrath—past, present, and future

Library of Congress Cataloging-in-Publication Data

McGrath, Michael E.
     Product development: success through product and cycle-time
excellence / Michael E. McGrath, Michael T. Anthony, Amram R.
Shapiro.
       p.   cm. —(The Electonic business series)
     Includes bibliographical references and index.
     ISBN 0-7506-9289-8
     1. Production engineering.   2. New products.   3. Production
planning.   I. Anthony, Michael T.   II. Shapiro, Amram R.
III. Title.   IV. Series.
TS176.M373   1992   92-25001
658.5'75—dc20   CIP

British Library Cataloguing in Publication Data
A catalogue record for this book is available from the British Library.

Butterworth–Heinemann
80 Montvale Avenue
Stoneham, MA 02180

10 9 8 7 6 5 4 3

Printed in the United States of America

Contents

Preface

During the late 1970s and throughout the 1980s, dramatic improvements in the manufacturing process began to change the competitive balance in many industries. The cost and quality advantages achieved through manufacturing-process improvements such as just-in-time (JIT) and total quality management (TQM) were so significant that all companies needed to change in order to remain competitive. In industries such as automotive and consumer electronics, Japanese companies leading these improvements climbed from secondary to dominant positions. In other industries, American and European competitors realized what was happening and began to catch up.

Since its founding in 1976, Pittiglio Rabin Todd & McGrath (PRTM) has become the leader in operations management consulting to technology-based industries. We have helped many companies in the United States and Europe to change the way they manufacture products, in many cases applying the so-called Japanese techniques of JIT and TQM. While some companies such as the ones we worked with were able to make these changes, others gave up manufacturing completely or simply went out of business.

In 1986 I realized that there was an obvious lesson to be learned. The next time there was a revolutionary change in one of the fundamental business processes, it would be better to be out ahead instead of catching up. PRTM, as the leading consulting firm to high-technology industries, was in a good position to identify and lead any future changes. Our extensive client base gave us good insights into how companies could change and the significance of improving the various areas of their operations.

In addition to working with our clients, we met with leading academics and researchers and looked into process improvements that Japanese companies were making in new areas. The result of all this was clear—the product development process would be the next major business revolution, and the strategic impact of this improvement would be even greater than that of JIT and quality in manufacturing.

We found that the opportunity and the challenge of this improvement were the same: product development was not being managed as a process. Managing it as a process presented a totally new opportunity. Defining and implementing the most effective product development process was the challenge. The process flow and the dynamics needed to be defined. New concepts needed to be developed in such areas as project team organization and structured development. Numerous techniques and frameworks needed to be adapted and devised. These all needed to come together in a way that could actually be implemented.

During 1986 and early 1987, we developed many of the necessary concepts and techniques, as well as much of the process definition. We refined and tested them over the next five years by working with selected clients. The companies we worked with were industry leaders that could see the strategic benefit in improving product development. They realized that many of the concepts were new and untested, but the concepts made sense, and our clients had confidence that we could make them work.

The result was a new approach to product development. PRTM refers to the process, concepts, techniques, and frameworks collectively known as Product And Cycle-time Excellence (PACE). Some of these are totally new. Some were successful in other areas and modified for product development. Others are derived from the best practices that we found during our studies and benchmarking. They were all put together into an integrated process for product development—PACE.

PACE is more than a process. It is also a goal and a philosophy—achieving excellence in the quality and success of new products, while simultaneously achieving the shortest time to market.

By the middle of 1992, PRTM had implemented PACE in more than 25 companies or divisions. Most of them are well-known technology-based companies that are perceived as leaders in their industries. They all achieved significant benefits in time to market and product success. Collectively, PACE has been successfully implemented on more than 150 new product development efforts.

In this book we set out to define the PACE process, concepts, techniques, and frameworks for product development. The success we have had in applying them leads us to believe they can benefit all companies doing product development. This book is intended to fill a void: the lack of any specific conceptual framework for the product development process.

The material for this book comes from our actual experience in making improvements in product development; as a firm this is more than 100 man-years worth of experience over the past six years. It is based on our training sessions and workshops, which have been conducted for several thousand product developers.

The first chapter explains why the product development process will be the battleground for the 1990s by clarifying the significant benefits to be achieved. It also looks at why these benefits have not yet been achieved. This leads into Chapter 2, which introduces PACE and provides an overview of PACE as an integrated process.

In Part II we define the seven interrelated elements of the PACE process. Each of these elements is covered in a separate chapter that explains specific concepts, techniques, and frameworks. Each chapter also explains why the element needs to be improved and provides illustrations of how it should work.

Finally, Part III addresses several aspects of implementation. Chapter 10 discusses the stages in the evolution of Product And Cycle-time Excellence that provide a road map for companies to see where they are now and where they can go. Chapter 11 on project team leadership addresses some specific issues on finding and developing the right product development leaders. Chapter 12 introduces the challenges of implementation.

We want to emphasize one cautionary note, however. While numerous examples throughout the book illustrate the concepts, this is not a "how to" book or cookbook. Implementing improvements to the product development process, or any complex process for that matter, requires skills beyond those which can be explained.

In preparing this book, Mike Anthony, Amram Shapiro, and I would like to thank the many people throughout PRTM who contributed their time, experience, and talent to helping in the completion of this book. While it is impossible to thank everyone by name, we would like to especially recognize the efforts of Jon McKay, who made significant contributions to the book when it was needed. We would also like to thank the PRTM support staff, which is world class.

Most of all, we would like to express our appreciation to the firm's clients. The challenges on which we work together have been a constant inspiration to us to push the state of the art even further.

Michael E. McGrath
Director, Pittiglio Rabin Todd & McGrath
Weston, Massachusetts

Introduction

1

The Battleground of the 1990s

If manufacturing was viewed as the industrial battleground of the late 1970s and 1980s, then product development is the battleground of the 1990s. The battle that started in the 70s, and continues today, was over lower-cost and higher-quality products. The battle starting now is over more, newer, and better products.

The advantages that come from reducing time to market and consistently developing better products are so significant that they will shift the competitive balance in favor of companies that can achieve them first. A company that can efficiently introduce more new products, react faster to market and technology changes, and develop superior products will win the battle with its competitors. The key to achieving these advantages is improving the product development process. This is why it will become the battleground of the 1990s.

Intriguingly, many similarities exist between the changes that took place in manufacturing in previous decades and the opportunity for improvement in the product development process. Each opportunity is significant enough to achieve a real competitive advantage, and both manufacturing and product development changes are sustainable through continual improvement. In each case, the opportunity stems from redefining the underlying process using new management concepts.

The competitive advantage achieved by improving product development comes about in several ways. Comprehending the full extent of the benefits to be gained helps us to understand the significance of the potential competitive advantage. It also begins to establish the performance criteria that companies should expect from their product development process.

Benefits of a More Effective Product Development Process

For almost all product-based companies, improving the product development process will be more beneficial than any other improvement. It will enable them to attain higher revenue than they otherwise would have. It will significantly improve the productivity of product development activities, and it will increase efficiencies in other operational areas within the company.

These benefits are the common result of an integrated set of improvements to the product development process, rather than a trade-off such as time for quality. Similarly, with manufacturing process improvements, quality or cycle-time improvements were not achieved at the expense of higher product cost. Instead, a higher quality process benefited all areas.

Increased Revenue

All companies can increase revenue by improving their product development process. In fact, in most companies this increase can be so significant that it can fuel revenue growth until competitors catch up by improving their own product development process. Alternatively, when competitors are able to improve their product development process first, a company will see a decline in revenue. This higher revenue comes about from increased product life-cycle revenue, increased market penetration, success in time-sensitive markets, and more successful products.

Increased product life-cycle revenue

In our experience, most companies can cut time to market in half with a better product development process. For example, the Codex division of Motorola cut its average product development time by 46% over a two-year period.[1] Similarly, Bolt Beranek and Newman dramatically reduced time to market by 50–60% for the first product developed with its new process.[2]

An improvement of this magnitude significantly increases revenue throughout a product's life cycle. Figure 1 illustrates how this happens. The lightly shaded curve represents a typical product life cycle of approximately four years, with a ramp-up in the begin-

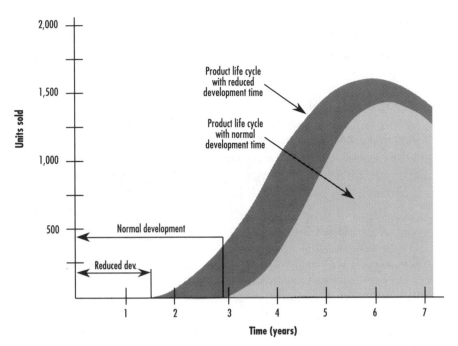

Figure 1. Product life cycle curves with normal and faster time to market.

ning, a peak after two and one-half years, and then a ramp-down until the product is terminated or replaced by a newer product.

During the introduction stage, sales of the product increase as most early adopters begin to buy it. Sales do not jump directly to the highest level because

- the broad base of customers may be reluctant to be the first to try new products
- buying decisions may take time
- many customers are interested in trying one before they buy many
- the product needs to technically demonstrate that it works
- the product needs to develop a reputation and image
- customers need to become aware of the product
- internal manufacturing and distribution need to ramp up

During the growth stage, sales climb substantially if the new product satisfies customers. Early adopters will continue purchasing a large number of products, and more conservative customers will begin to follow their lead. New competitors may enter the market at this stage, and existing competitors will introduce new product features in an attempt to expand the total market.

Eventually sales growth slows as the product enters a state of relative maturity. In many industries, the product life cycle peaks in two and one-half to four years. After a period of little or no growth, sales eventually decrease in the face of improved products from competitors or technical leapfrogging by replacement products. At this point, most companies either cease manufacturing and selling the product or offer a new product in its place.

When a new product is brought to market earlier, than typically, it not only generates revenue in the initial period but maintains higher sales throughout the product life cycle. This can be seen graphically in Figure 1, where the darker-shaded curve shows product sales with a reduction of 45% in development time. Recognizing this corrects a frequent misconception that the only sales difference occurs during the time period from when the product could have been on the market to when it was actually introduced. While there are earlier revenues, there also are higher revenues at every stage of the product's life. In fact, whenever a product is released to market, it follows a life-cycle curve. Incremental revenue accumulates every year until the peak is reached, and the peak is frequently higher for the earlier entry. Only in the latest stage of the life cycle may the rates converge.

Increased market penetration as a result of being first to market

A product that is first to market has the potential to establish a leadership position in the market. This potential arises from three sources: being the first to respond to a new market opportunity, being the first to apply new technology, or being able to respond more quickly to changes in the market. The vice chairman of Conner Peripherals, Bill Schroeder, states this succinctly: "The first guy to market cleans up."[3]

Apple Computer was the first to respond to the opportunity for improving ease of use in personal computers with the Lisa and then the Macintosh computers. The Lisa did not succeed because of its high price, but Apple was able to deliver the same icon-based user interface in the lower-priced Macintosh before any other similar interface hit the market. This enabled it to significantly differentiate its personal computer and capture a specific segment of the market. If another personal computer company had beaten Apple to market with a user-friendly graphic interface, the Macintosh would have been much less successful.

A product that is early to market can also impact technical as well as informal standards. Technical standards include common formats, software standards, and protocols. In some cases these technical standards can even be protected, as Intel and Polaroid have been able to do. In such industries as pharmaceuticals, so dependent on patent protection for high margins, an additional year before the product comes off patent may be worth a fortune. Informal standards such as the form factor or feel of the product can also be important. Gary Tooker, president of Motorola, points out that the form factor for the company's portable hand-held phone has established a standard in the industry for "feel" because it was first to market.

In some volume-sensitive industries, the competitor who captures significant market share first is likely to be the low-cost producer. Costs continue to decline with experience, and second-tier players can never be as profitable.

Being first to market, however, does not always guarantee success. EMI developed the original CAT scanner but did not have the support and service necessary to be successful. Competitors such as GE and Technicon offered better service and support and were capable of developing a successful product. In 1979 EMI received the Nobel prize for the CAT scanner, but the company had to be acquired in order to be saved.

Success in time-sensitive markets

In some industries, the windows of market opportunity remain open for only a short time. In these cases the ability to make any sales at all depends on time to market. Customer-specific components such as custom semiconductor devices fall into this category. If a company can develop the component in time to be designed into the customer's end product, then it may be able to get that customer's business; if it can't, a competitor gets it. Time to market and predictability of supply become sources of significant competitive advantage in industries such as these.

The computer workstation market is another example of a time-sensitive market. Most workstations are purchased by systems integrators, companies that integrate their own proprietary equipment and applications software into a system that they sell to specific users. While the life cycle of a new generation of workstations may be three to four years, the system integrator selects the workstation around which it will build its system very quickly after the release of a new generation.

Sun Microsystems believes that it has only a year to convince customers to buy its new products. If customers select Sun in that first year, they are likely to continue to order products for another three or four years. If Sun is late by a year, however, the company feels it has missed the market. At the end of 1985 Sun introduced the Sun 3 product line to replace the Sun 2 product line introduced in 1983. The Sun 3 was developed in approximately one year, giving Sun a significant advantage. Because it came to market sooner, more systems integrators selected it as the basis for their systems. Sun's revenue skyrocketed from $115 million in 1985 to more than $1 billion in three years. Sun's market share also leaped from 16 to 28%, while that of its major competitor, Apollo, dropped from 51 to 31%.

More successful products

Our experience in improving product development processes has also shown dramatic improvement in the success of new products. This stems from some of the aspects of a better process such as the synergy of having people work more closely together, the design improvements of a more methodical process, and the impact of better decision making. Marketing and engineering, for example, can make better trade-offs and find new opportunities. When this is combined with the discipline of a more structured process, it helps to set the right priorities for the product.

Sometimes overlooked as a benefit is how shorter time to market provides an advantage in defining product requirements. The opportunity and requirements for a new product are defined at the beginning of a product development project. The market can change, however, during the time it takes to develop the product.

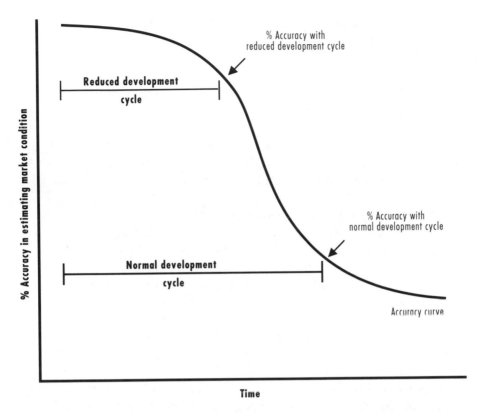

Figure 2. Increased accuracy in anticipating customer requirements comes from faster time to market.

Customers may become interested in new features. Prices may drop. Competitors may introduce new, more innovative products. A shorter product development cycle reduces the interval during which market conditions can change while the product is being developed.

As Figure 2 shows, the accuracy in estimating market conditions declines further in the future, usually with a precipitous drop at some point. While the slope of this curve varies, the shorter the horizon, the greater the accuracy. A shorter development cycle also enables a company to respond more rapidly to emerging market opportunities. With product development flexibility, a company can be much more market oriented and respond much more quickly to customer needs.

Improved Product Development Productivity

Product development productivity does not come from working people harder. Motivating developers to work day and night only temporarily increases capacity. Increased product development productivity is derived from shorter cycle times, less development waste, better resource utilization, and the ability to attract the best people. Again, the parallels to recent improvements in manufacturing should be obvious.

Shorter development cycle times

Most product development investments are run-rate based, meaning that a certain number of people work a product development project until it is completed. For example, 20 people may work on developing a new product for three years. Development costs correlate highly to cycle time: if the cycle time is reduced, development costs are lower. This is the same relationship between cost and cycle time that exists in manufacturing. The relationship between project cost and development cycle time is shown in Figure 3.

With an improved process, cycle time is reduced and project costs go down. In the previous example, if the project could be

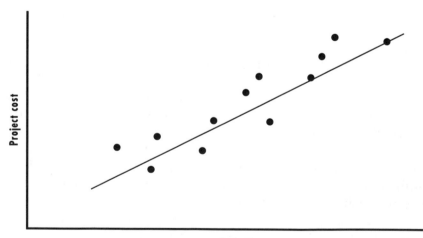

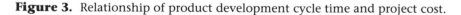

Figure 3. Relationship of product development cycle time and project cost.

completed in one and one and one-half years (half the time), it would not require 40 people (although it may require a few more than 20 to remove some constraints). Therefore, the project cost would be lower. This cost reduction, while related to the reduction in cycle time, is not directly proportional because other costs such as capital equipment, tooling, and outside expenses may not be reduced with shorter cycle time. We have found that a 50% reduction in product development cycle time typically leads to direct reduction of development costs of between 30 and 35%.

The resources saved through increased productivity permit reinvestment in additional product development to bring more new products to market, or a company can reduce the total amount of money that it spends on developing new products. Some companies have combined these cycle-time/cost-reduction benefits by increasing development activity along with reducing the money they spend. Most have increased their new product output.

Less development waste

Some cancellations or significant redirections of product development projects are to be expected in any development activity. Too often, however, projects are canceled or refocused quite late, after significant investments have been made. It is astonishing how often cancellation or refocusing could have taken place much earlier. The necessary information was either known or knowable, but nobody asked the right questions or made the right decisions. One company, for example, invested $40 million in a product and then canceled it after prototypes were working because the market opportunity was insufficient. This decision could have been made after spending only five percent of that amount, if the proper market analysis had been done.

Our benchmarks have shown that companies that make decisions earlier invest approximately half as much in products that are not brought to market. For example, while the average company in one industry segment we studied spent 36% of its development on products that never came to market, companies that made decisions earlier spent only 20%. Put another way, companies with a better decision-making process can spend less on product development and achieve comparable output because they waste less on products that do not come to market.

Better resource utilization

Companies often miss project milestones because key tasks are delayed waiting for the right people to do them. Some projects are canceled well into development because the development resources are needed elsewhere. People bounce back and forth from project to project, with resulting drops in effectiveness and increases in needed coordination. Companies typically launch more product development projects than they have capacity for and then are surprised when projects fall behind schedule. Ineffective resource allocation is frequently the underlying cause.

Here again the analogy to manufacturing improvement applies. Traditional manufacturing management encouraged companies to launch as much work as possible to keep the factory highly utilized. This led to bulging work-in-process inventory, schedule slippage, and increased overhead. Until the emphasis changed to cycle-time reduction, people lost sight that the goal was not to start as much as possible but to finish as much as possible.

Just as the implementation of just-in-time manufacturing clearly exposes production bottlenecks, the implementation of a high-performance product development process clearly exposes real resource needs and skill bottlenecks. Managing these constraints enables a company to set the priorities necessary to implement its strategy, match the mix of development resources to its needs, and increase overall productivity.

Better ability to attract and retain technical talent

The most capable and creative people are almost always the most productive. This is particularly true in product development, where creativity and skill are essential.

With a rapid product development process, a company is in a much better position to both attract and retain key development talent. Product development professionals, whether they are technical gurus or project managers, are more interested in a work environment where their efforts result more frequently in successful new products. Such an environment allows them to work on more projects during their career. Conversely, if they work in an environment where their efforts stretch out over a long period of time, they become frustrated and inevitably look for new work environments. Given the importance of exceptional technical talent in the product development process, attracting and retaining the best people can become a significant long-term advantage.

Operational Efficiencies

Improving product development can also achieve operational benefits—especially in manufacturing and service—by designing a product to make operations easier or more efficient. More predictable product completion dates also improve the efficiency of the product-release process.

Design for manufacturability, serviceability, etc.

Operational efficiencies in manufacturing, distribution, and service can be achieved by better product designs. This focus is typically incorporated in such design methods as design for manufacturing and assembly (DFMA), design for international (DFI), and design for serviceability (DFS).

NCR (Manufacturing) Ltd. in Dundee, Scotland, the world's leader in automated teller machines (ATMs), employed DFMA when it redesigned the money cassette for its ATM, replacing the old aluminum cassette with one made from polycarbonate injection moldings and die castings. The new cassette was designed to be assembled with a high degree of robotic assembly. In the end, the redesigned cassette was so simple to assemble that it could even be done manually at low cost. NCR thus reduced product cost by 44% and assembly time by 70%. Additionally, customers viewed the new cassette as a significant improvement because it proved to be much more durable than the previous metal design.

Higher-quality products

High product quality is an essential element of product excellence. Baldrige award–winner Motorola is noted for the success of its six-sigma quality program, a statistical term denoting 3.4 defects per million operations. Motorola's Codex division implemented six-sigma as part of its improved product development process. Codex achieved this by integrating specific quality requirements into all steps of a consistent design process and through a decision process that requires achievement of quality goals before a product is released. Codex has actually delayed products that did not meet these stringent quality hurdles, even though the products were functioning and customers were awaiting delivery.

Motorola's Paging Products Division achieved greatly improved quality and reduced cost for its pager product with what the company called the Bandit project. This involved redesigning the product to make it manufacturable on an automated production line. Achieving the demanding quality goals involved making design trade-offs. The original design placed all the components on a single side of the printed circuit board in order to make manufacturing easier, but this required the components to be so tightly packed that it was impossible to achieve high quality levels. The redesign placed components on both sides, and production was automated to accommodate two-sided assembly.

Apple Computer learned the lesson of product-design quality the hard way with the Apple III. The first production units worked only when the cover was removed. The connectors between the main board and the memory board were easily corroded, leading the computer to forget what it was doing. The clock display frequently malfunctioned, and the lines on the printed circuit board would short circuit. Apple redesigned this model and corrected many of the shortcomings, but the product never recovered and was eventually withdrawn from the market as a failure. Apple was able to survive this quality debacle, but many other companies having similar problems were not as fortunate.

Lower engineering change order costs

The costs of implementing engineering change orders (ECOs) caused by design problems can frequently be higher than most companies realize. For example, one company estimated that 10% of its direct labor was involved in implementing ECOs. In fact, in some of our benchmarking we found that more than half of the companies surveyed incurred ECO costs that were greater than 10% of the original development costs. ECOs are frequently caused by the rush to market, which often leads companies to introduce products too early.

ECOs can increase other costs as well. For example, the service costs caused by such problems can be enormous. One highly innovative blood-analyzer system introduced too early required replacement of parts and subsystems equal in cost to the selling price of the unit in all systems installed in the first year. At another company the sales force spent 80% of its time baby-sitting a new product. This kept current customers pacified, but who was developing new customers?

The number of ECOs after product release is directly related to the quality of product design. The product development process drives the quality of product design through such practices as structured development, design reviews, and concurrent engineering.

Improved predictability of release

Many operational activities take place just before and after the release of a new product. These include market launch activities, acquisition of components for the new product, and the phase out of older products being replaced. Some of these activities require decisions to be made months or even a year or more before the new-product release date. The failure to accurately predict product-release dates has caused a precipitous drop in revenue for many companies, which ended up unable to ship even the older products to customers.

In some cases, companies are forced to release products before they are ready. A manager at a company we know that had this problem put it this way: "Our products don't get launched; they escape!"

The benefits of reliable release dates vary by company and situation. If a company does not have confidence in the release date of a new product, it usually stocks up on additional inventory of older products—just in case. These are later written off if the new product is on schedule. If a company prepares its sales force—or worse, its customers—for a new product and then misses its expected release date, a significant revenue impact will occur. Lotus Software experienced this in 1985 when it missed its schedule for releasing Jazz, its integrated software product for the Macintosh.

Why Haven't Companies Already Achieved These Benefits?

Despite significant benefits, most companies have not yet made major improvements to their product development process, and important but generally untapped opportunities like this are rare. That is why improving product development is a unique opportunity—one that can upset the competitive balance of many industries.

Why hasn't the product development process been improved? We believe that the answer is in the follow reasons:

1. *Product development has not been viewed, managed, or taught as a process.* Traditionally, product development has been looked upon as an art—products were created by a mixture of genius and inspiration. It was not something that could be managed; it just happened.

Much of the previous literature focused on the mysteries of creativity and human communication. This work is interesting, but it implies that product development cannot be managed, only a suitable climate provided. Structure and active management needn't stifle innovation; they provide boundaries that focus creativity and empowerment based on clear-cut responsibilities. Structure doesn't impede product development. It merely clarifies the process. Then the creativity starts.

Most companies have not invested in improving their product development process because it was never managed as a process. In frequent meetings with company executives, we ask the following questions after citing the benefits of improving the product development process:

- How much did you invest in improving your manufacturing *process* through manufacturing systems such as material requirements planning (MRP), techniques such as just-in-time (JIT) and total quality control (TQC), production process improvements such as production or manufacturing engineering, and training in process-improvement skills? The answers usually indicated that they have made significant investments in these areas.
- How much do you invest in improving the product development *process* through process engineering, implementing new techniques, organizational improvement, and training? The answer in all cases has been "little or none."

These executives quickly realize that they have not been investing in improving their most essential business process.

Product development *is* a process. Inputs such as market opportunities and technology go into the process, and products result. The process can be defined, structured, and managed. There are similarities from one development project to another, and, like any process, it can be continually improved. Most importantly, the competitor with a superior process has an advantage.

2. *The necessary concepts and techniques have only recently been developed.* The revolution in manufacturing required new concepts for managing manufacturing in a completely different way. Innovative methods such as just-in-time production, new philosophies such as total quality management and vendor partnering, and supporting techniques, such as pull mechanisms, and set-up time reduction, provided the foundation for companies implementing this new manufacturing process.

The concepts, philosophies, and techniques for managing the product development process lag far behind those for manufacturing. Until recently there had been few advances in the process of developing products. PACE (Product And Cycle-time Excellence) is an integrated approach to product development that addresses this. It includes new management concepts, techniques, and frameworks for achieving high-performance product development.

3. *The improvement usually requires a cultural change.* Improving the product development process usually involves moving toward a performance-oriented approach where the focus becomes teamwork, rapid decision making, and clear responsibility. This orientation presents a cultural change for many companies.

Cultural change, even when desired, is difficult to implement. It cuts across all functions horizontally and all levels vertically. Attempts to edict improvements that require a completely different way of doing things rarely work. While cultural change usually evolves over time or comes as the result of an upheaval, successful companies have been able to change their culture to implement improvements. Hewlett Packard with JIT and Motorola with quality are well-known examples of this type of cultural change. Because it is so difficult to achieve, however, it has stopped many companies that want to change the way they develop products.

4. *Cross-functional changes are difficult to make from within.* Product development is a cross-functional process, and not only are the improvements cross functional, but much of the

emphasis is on lowering functional barriers. Companies that have attempted cross-functional change have found it is difficult with internal initiatives.

If a vice president in one function leads the change, for example, then everyone believes that he or she is biased to make tasks easier for his or her own function; and in many companies there is a long history of this actually happening. If the change is initiated by a multifunctional group or committee, it is typically bogged down by many of the problems of group consensus. Frequently, outside assistance is necessary to successfully implement cross-functional change.

5. *The changes are extensive.* The product development process is complex, and hundreds or even thousands of changes may be required to improve it. Most of them are small, but a few are very large. Nevertheless, they all need to be coordinated since many are interdependent. Deciding on making the numerous changes and coordinating their implementation can overwhelm companies that are inexperienced or not committed to the change. They try, but fail, and the resulting frustration makes the situation even worse.

Competitive Advantage

Individually, the benefits of increased revenue, improved product development productivity, and operational efficiencies are compelling. Taken together they provide a significant competitive advantage. Companies able to achieve this advantage will grow faster, be more profitable, and succeed against competitors who can't.

The combined advantages open the possibility for new competitive strategies. A company with these advantages could inundate its competitors with new products. Toshiba attempted this strategy by blitzing the laptop computer market with an avalanche of new products, addressing virtually every market niche. In fact, by 1991, Toshiba had discontinued more laptops than some of its competitors had launched. Faced with this onslaught, customers may consider these competitors also-rans because their product development cycle is longer than the product life cycle established by Toshiba.[4]

Alternatively, a company with these advantages could profitably develop products that its competitors could only match at a loss or it could choose to be significantly more profitable on the same level of new product investment. The strategic possibilities are many, and they will be the basis for the new competitive battles of the 1990s.

These benefits are not theoretical. Companies are achieving them today. Almost any company can achieve them, and most executives realize that they must. Most executives we talk to are disappointed in their product development process. Most, as revealed by our benchmarking studies, believe that their companies could reduce time to market by at least one-third.

Summary

The product development process will be the battleground of the 1990s, a battle that will change the competitive balance of some industries for the following reasons:

- An improved the product development process can increase revenue by increasing product life-cycle revenue, improving market penetration, enabling success in time-sensitive markets, and creating more successful products.
- An improved product development process can increase productivity by shortening development cycle times, reducing wasted development, improving resource utilization, and attracting technical talent.
- It can also improve other operational efficiencies by incorporating design for manufacturability, encouraging higher-quality products, reducing the number of ECOs, and improving the predictability of release.
- Achieved together, the benefits of an improved product development process can establish a significant competitive advantage.
- The magnitude of improvement is significant—for example, most companies can cut time to market in half.
- For several reasons, product development remains an untapped opportunity, mainly because it has not been viewed as a process, and it is very difficult to change.
- Because it is a significant and still untapped opportunity, improving the product development process will become the competitive battleground of the 1990s.

References

1. Rick Whiting, "Product Development as a Process," *Electronic Business*, June 17, 1991.
2. *BBN Communications News Release*, Oct. 8, 1991, p. 4.
3. Rick Whiting, "Product Development as a Process," *Electronic Business*, June 17, 1991, p. 31.
4. Gary Hamel and C.K. Prahalad, "Corporate Imagination and Expeditionary Marketing," *Harvard Business Review*, July–Aug. 1991.

2

PACE: An Integrated Process for Product And Cycle-time Excellence

The only sustainable source of product advantage is a superior product development process. Advantages based on a brilliant design, fortunate timing, a clever product strategy, or a lucky break cannot be sustained. Such factors cannot be relied upon to consistently create successful products over the long term. An inferior development process will make advantages based on such factors short-lived. A superior process will leverage them powerfully.

Here again we turn to the analogy with manufacturing. While such factors as skilled workers, modern equipment, and low-cost labor can provide a temporary advantage, the only sustainable source of manufacturing advantage is a superior manufacturing process. Realizing this, many companies have invested in improving their manufacturing processes.

Material requirements planning (MRP) became the primary architecture for the manufacturing process during the 1970s. It integrated various elements of the manufacturing process, including master production scheduling, inventory management, purchasing, work-order tracking, and bill-of-material control. Later this architecture evolved to become manufacturing resource planning (MRP II), which integrated even more elements into the process of manufacturing.

In the 1980s Japanese companies introduced manufacturing processes based on the principles of just-in-time (JIT), short cycle times, and total quality management. Companies that made these improvements were able to achieve a competitive advantage in manufacturing through a superior process. To improve their manufacturing processes they invested in new techniques, systems, organizational changes, and process engineering.

When product development is not viewed as a process, there is little consistency across projects. Each project team decides how to organize itself and what steps it will follow in developing its product. Little common terminology is shared among developers or managers. For example, a term such as *functional specification* may be used to mean something entirely different from one project to another. Without a common process, senior managers may have no consistent basis on which to decide what projects go forward.

Product development is a process. It takes insights into customer needs and wants, combines them with the company's technologies and skills, and then transforms opportunities into products. The process is generally similar for all products developed within a company. Although there are product differences, the approach to project-team organization, project management, decision making, planning, and indeed many of the specific steps can be consistent. In fact, there can even be a high degree of similarity in the product development process from company to company.

This similarity enables the product development process to be structured, defined, and managed. Companies can develop a common process so that each project team does not have to invent its own. They can invest in improving the process so that all projects reap the benefits, and like other business processes, a similar product development process can be engineered in general for all companies. Best practices can be applied across many companies, and a general structure for product development can be modified for each. As a result, a company does not need to invent its own process from scratch.

PRTM's Product And Cycle-time Excellence (PACE) is a general model for the product development process. It is a proven approach based on an understanding of best practices and extensive experience. PACE integrates the major elements that constitute product development and corrects the deficiencies that exist in many product development processes today.

The Product Development Process

In developing and refining the PACE approach, we have studied in detail more than one hundred product development projects at numerous companies in order to understand the problems that typically arise in development. These projects represented almost a $1 billion investment in new products and involved more than 3,500 people. We found that most problems and disappointments were the result of deficiencies in the product development processes. We also found a great deal of commonality among the problems. In particular, the process deficiencies that were the underlying causes of the problems occurred in many of the product development processes that we evaluated.

The process for product development can be segmented into seven interrelated elements. In each of these elements we identified some common deficiencies. The PACE process provides the approaches, techniques, and methods for overcoming deficiencies in each of these elements of the product development process. Following is a description of the seven interrelated elements of the product development process, a summary of some of the common deficiencies, and a brief definition of the PACE process for that element of product development. The PACE process for each of these elements is described in detail in subsequent chapters.

Decision Making

All companies have a decision-making process for new products, although they may not recognize it as an explicitly defined process. Somebody eventually makes decisions or the decisions become no longer necessary. Where the decision-making process is unreliable, delays are common. For example, when many managers must be persuaded to adopt a product concept off-line before a project can get started, differences in opinion among these managers are not easily resolved. We have seen some good opportunities ignored simply because the product champions didn't understand how to make the informal decision process work.

One company we worked with had an ambiguous new product decision process that was typical of many situations we have seen. Project reviews had deteriorated to a series of presentations to varied audiences. Many people attended and asked numerous questions, but senior management eventually avoided the reviews. These were not decision-making sessions. The right information was not presented. The reviews were not given at the right point in the development. Decision makers were not involved, nor were there any mechanisms to force timely decisions.

Not all explicitly defined processes are effective, however. Some are poorly defined or have not been properly implemented. Poorly designed or not properly implemented, a formal process can be an administrative hindrance to product development. Instead of becoming the beat that drives product development, the decision-making process unnecessarily consumes an extensive amount of time with little benefit.

In our reviews of product development we have seen other problems in decision making. Typically these include deficiencies similar to the following:

- Senior management unconsciously delays or revises decisions because it is not clear who should make the decision or what type of consensus is needed.
- Poor decisions result from the inadequacy of information or level of detail presented to senior management. The right questions are not answered at the right time.
- Decision points are not defined so that reviews occur at the appropriate milestones; typically, reviews at regular time periods, instead of milestones, are not effective for decision making.
- Resources are overcommitted to the point that it becomes impossible to get anything done on schedule.
- Funding for product development projects is not clearly approved through decisions by those authorized to approve new products and set priorities.
- Decisions are made too late—frequently after the product is already designed.
- Strategic decisions are made in frustration by developers because senior management has not made them.

In the PACE process, new product decision making is implemented through a Phase Review Process that requires decisions at specifically defined points during development. A product development project must achieve clearly defined objectives in the expected time frame in order to get approval to continue into the next phase.

Product Approval Committee (PAC) is a term used to describe the senior management group within a division or company that has the specific authority and responsibility to make major new product decisions. The PAC has the authority to approve or reject new products by funding or modifying them at specific decision points in the development cycle. It is responsible for implementing the company's strategy through product development activities and therefore has the resource-allocation authority to drive new product development.

The PAC makes decisions and allocates resources through the Phase Review Process. Without such a process it is virtually impossible for senior management to effectively guide new product development. Simply having a Phase Review Process (or something similar such as a tollgate process or stage-development process), however, is not enough. A poor definition, improper implementation, or incompatibility with other necessary elements of the development process can make the Phase Review Process ineffective.

The Phase Review Process plays another important role in product development. Through it the PAC empowers the project team to develop the project on a phase-by-phase basis. The project team defines its recommendations for the product, presents a plan to develop it, and requests the resources required for the next phase of development. If the PAC approves the team's recommendations, it empowers the team with the authority, responsibility and resources required to implement the next phase of its plan.

Project Team Organization

In our reviews we found that most companies did not have a clearly defined approach for organizing product development efforts. Many tended to follow variations of their functional organizations in establishing product development teams, usually because they did not have a clearly defined philosophy for project teams. As a result, communication, coordination, and decision making were inefficient and confused.

One company typified this with numerous managers participating in product development meetings only when they had the time or when a specific issue made it a priority. Because this approach created poor results, the company tried different ways to fix it. A program-management department was established to monitor schedules and commitments in order to identify who was supposed to do what and whether it was done. Later, each function assigned its own project manager to every major project. Neither of these approaches worked very well. They only increased non-value-added effort, which was already too high.

Some companies tried to establish project team organizations, but they were not truly effective. The following are typical of the reasons that we have seen for this:

- Confusion results when the responsibilities and authorities of the teams are not clearly defined.
- Teams are ineffective because they are not really empowered to accomplish the objectives; in some cases they are given the responsibility but not the authority or resources.
- Concurrent engineering is lacking because some functions and skills are not properly integrated into the team's activities.
- Ineffective project leadership stems from several different reasons: inexperienced project leaders, a poorly defined role for project leadership within the company, inadequate training, and a flawed definition of the project team organization.
- Project teams can not achieve results because they lack the staff and skills to do it; frequently resources are moved from team to team without any clear decision.
- Conflict and confusion arise between the project team and the functional organization because the way they work together is not clearly defined; usually the emphasis continues to be the function rather than the project.
- Ineffective teams result from confusion over what the members are supposed to do; for example, team members think they are functional reviewers and not actual contributors.

Project-team organization is one of the most essential elements of the product development process. An effective project team vastly improves communication, coordination and decision making. In our reviews we found that all of the popular project-team approaches were ineffective in ways similar to those described. As part of the PACE process, we developed a new approach that takes the best aspects of other approaches and overcomes the drawbacks. We call it the Core Team approach to project team organization.

The Core Team is a small cross-functional project team that has the specific authority to develop a particular product. A typical Core Team has five to eight members, each dedicated to the project. Members have the authority and responsibility to manage all of the tasks associated with the development of the product. Specific tasks are divided among the Core Team members, and each performs these tasks using staff assigned to the project. Core Team members have the responsibility for managing specific tasks, supervising the work of those assigned to them, interfacing with functional areas, and collectively making decisions as part of the Core Team. The PAC empowers the Core Team with this responsibility and authority at each phase of the development effort through the Phase Review Process. Each Core Team has a leader who guides and directs the team.

The Structure of Development Activity

Development activity is the actual work that takes place to develop a new product. The structure of this activity defines what is done, the sequence of activities, their interdependencies, and the terminology for development. In our reviews we found three general categories of deficiencies in the structure of development activity: companies without any defined structure for product development, those with procedure manuals for a structure that was not followed, and those with structure that did not improve or speed up development.

In the first case, companies that have not structured their development activities must repeatedly reinvent the wheel during product development. Each project team is expected to define the process that it will follow, and each project team does development differently, even if it is performing the same or similar tasks. The burden on the product development team is putting the development process in place. This obviously takes additional time, and the team learns by its mistakes, but project teams throughout the company keep making the same mistakes.

In the second case, an engineer or a staff person typically defines the development process. This definition usually is issued in a procedure book with the naive expectation that everyone will follow it. Of course they don't, and in most cases it is better that they don't. Projects teams again put in place their own product development process.

In the third case, development activities are defined and followed, but the process is inherently inefficient. Surprisingly, when they formalize their process, many companies simply document what they are already doing, even if it is ineffective. As a result, they institutionalize their problems.

In our reviews of development activity, we have found the following deficiencies to be common:

- Continuous revision of products that results from undisciplined development activity; for example, product definitions that keep changing after development is well underway.
- Inadequate project planning and preparation because there is no vision of where the development activity is going.
- Poor execution of development that stems directly from a lack of common terminology and the understanding it brings; without common terminology miscommunication is frequent.
- Definition of product development activity that is so detailed that it makes development inefficient. Typically the definition lacks any structure or layers.
- Slow development that results from a bureaucratic process with multiple sign-offs at every step.
- The absence of concurrent engineering because it is not accommodated in the definition of development activity.
- Project schedules that are inaccurate because cycle-time guidelines are not defined for development activity.
- The lack of continuous improvement of the product development process because the responsibility for it has not been assigned.

In the PACE process the Core Team develops a product using structured development. A structured process ensures that a consistent process is followed for development, thus avoiding the need for each project team to invent its own process. A common structured process also enables the use of common cycle-time guidelines and provides continuous improvement.

In the PACE approach, a structured development process consists of several layers. Within the framework provided by the Phase Review Process there are typically 15–20 major steps that define a company's process for developing products. Each of these steps is then broken into 10–30 tasks that define how each step is done within that company. The tasks define standard cycle times for each step so that steps can be used as building blocks for scheduling, estimating resource requirements, planning, and management.

Each task may be broken down further into various activities. The number of activities within each step varies from several to as many as 30 or 40, according to the nature of the task. Generally, steps and tasks apply consistently from project to project, while activities tend to be project-specific.

Product Strategy

Product strategy is the starting point for the development of new products. It defines the types of products a company wants to develop, how it differentiates these products from those of its competitors, how it introduces new technology into its products, and the priorities it establishes for developing new products.

Products selected for development should be consistent with overall product strategy, but often this is not the case. Frequently, product strategy has not been clearly developed and articulated, even though there may have been informal discussions throughout the organization. Without a clear product strategy, developers must guess about it as they propose and execute new product development. They learn what fits and what doesn't by trial and error, which is wasteful.

Sometimes we have found that the disconnection between product strategy and development projects is so profound that the former is a wish list without any impact on project selection. At one company, for example, the overriding strategic objective was seen as the development of many new products. Without more guidance than that, or some framework for evaluating product ideas and setting priorities, dozens of projects were started simultaneously on the initiative of individual developers or their managers. Most of them were never completed or, despite technical success, were never commercialized. "If I'd known what they were working on," the CEO told us, "I'd have stopped them sooner. Most of their projects didn't fit our strategy."

Our experience has shown the following typical deficiencies in the setting and communication of product strategy:

- Mediocre products are developed because the company does not effectively evaluate its opportunities; typically it does not use any frameworks to evaluate and prioritize product-line plans and new product-line opportunities.
- A product strategy is outdated because it focuses on today's needs, not future customer needs and market trends.

- Noncompetitive products result from a product strategy that is internally, not customer, driven; typically, competitive analysis is shallow and competitive positioning is unclear.
- Actual product development differs from what was intended because there is no articulation of a product strategy vision to guide those working on product development.

Contrary to many popular beliefs, product strategy is not derived by a blinding flash of innovation. Nor is it hundreds of pages of market analysis with charts and graphs. Digital Equipment Corporation for example, outlined one of the most successful product strategies in computer history with a three-page memo defining the future architecture of the VAX platform. Product strategy is a rigorous process to define a plan for new products based on understanding the opportunities created by the intersection of changes in the marketplace, advances in technology, and competitive positioning.

Within PACE, product strategy provides the framework used by the PAC to make decisions and set priorities in the Phase Review Process, and it establishes guidelines for the Core Team in defining products. Product strategy includes defining the opportunities for expanding current product lines and innovating new product lines.

Although specific product strategy processes vary by company— based on its approach to business strategy, its organization, its industry and competition, and so on—there are a few generic concepts and useful frameworks. The PACE product strategy element addresses these concerns with frameworks to identify opportunities both to expand current product lines and to target opportunities to innovate new product lines, concepts for competitively positioning products, and understanding the impact of technological change on product strategy.

Technology Management

Technology management is part of the overall product development process but needs to be implemented differently. The function of technology management is to identify opportunities for applying new technology, determine the core technologies critical to success, and initiate technology-development projects that further the company's core competencies and benefit multiple products.

We have found that some technology-based companies become so focused on product development that they overlook managing their underlying technology, and as a result, they end up developing technology as a subproject within product development. In other cases, companies do not really manage their underlying technologies. Some of the troubled development projects we reviewed ran into technical difficulties because the company didn't realize that it lacked some of the fundamental technical expertise to develop the product.

Product development relies on technology, whether internally developed or licensed or otherwise acquired from outside the organization; including from key suppliers. Timely access to fully usable technology requires identification of present and future core technologies because developing technology and other approaches to preferred access takes time. This cannot be done by forcing development project teams to create or acquire the necessary core technologies while they are developing a product. The degree of risk in a development project is that of its riskiest indispensable element. If that element is core technology development, the uncertainty and delay can be enormous.

One company, for example, didn't understand technology management. Research and development (R&D) was working on many varied technologies to be useful "three to ten years from now." Yet most of this work did not leverage the company's technology base. Consequently, its key technologies became mature. Starved for research dollars, core technologies imbedded in today's designs quickly became obsolete, and the company had to invest heavily to catch up.

In our reviews of product development, we found the following deficiencies in technology management to be common:

- Product development delays caused by technical surprises that could be avoided with better technical preparation.
- Deterioration of technical competencies because the company fails to invest in current and future core technologies.
- Unnecessarily long lead times for product development because technology development is not distinguished from product development.

- Product development failures due to the level of technical risk in product development projects not being managed.

The technology management element within PACE focuses on the interrelationship of product development and technology. It clarifies the distinction between product development and technology development and defines the interface between the two. Additionally, it describes a useful technique, technology unbundling, for developing technology strategy.

Design Techniques and Automated Development Tools

Design techniques such as quality function deployment (QFD), design for assembly (DFA), and design for manufacturability (DFM) can enhance the success of a product and achieve related operating efficiencies. None of these techniques alone, however, will solve all product development issues.

One large, multidivisional high-technology company, for example, selected QFD as its ultimate solution. It invested heavily to train the entire company in the design technique. Internal QFD experts and advisors were developed to spread the gospel. After nine months with no improvement in product development, the group was dissolved. The QFD technique was unfairly blamed because people expected a technique to make up for lack of an overall integrated approach.

During the past five to ten years, a number of new automated design tools have been developed that can significantly aid the product development process. These include computer aided design (CAD), software development tools such as computer aided software engineering (CASE), simulation tools, and tools for project planning, scheduling, and decision making. Again, none of them in and of itself provides a complete solution. They can help make a process more productive, but they require a framing process to begin with.

Regarding the use of these techniques and tools, we have found that many companies generally err in one of two ways: either they are not applying the right techniques and tools, or they are applying them ineffectively because they do not have an overall product development process. Specifically, we have seen the following problems to be common:

- Design techniques are ineffective because they don't fit well into an unclear product development process.
- A particular design technique such as QFD doesn't solve all product development problems, causing disappointment.
- New products are not manufacturable or serviceable because the proper design techniques were not used.
- Product development takes longer than it should because automated tools are not being applied.
- Automated development tools don't work well because the product definition keeps changing after it has been designed.

The PACE process does not define new techniques or tools; the design technique and automated tool element within PACE focuses on applying the right technique or tool, at the right time, and within the context of an overall product development process. It outlines a number of design techniques and automated development tools and shows how they fit into the process. QFD is focused on in more detail because of the integral role it plays within the early phases of product development. In particular, a variation of QFD, simplified quality function deployment (S-QFD), is introduced.

Cross-Project Management

Finally, the need for better management of certain factors across all product development becomes apparent after companies have eliminated deficiencies in the project-based aspects of product development. At that time conflicts across projects are more easily seen, and cross-project decisions can be made more effectively. Cross-project management and continuous improvement become the next priority.

With regard to cross-project management, we have found several common issues:

- Development project delays that stem from overallocated resources. Frequently this is caused by an ineffective resource scheduling system.

- Inefficient functional interfaces to the improved product development process because they have not been properly integrated.
- Product development that is out of balance with development skills.
- Product development that is out of balance with company objectives for growth, product mix, or short- or long-range emphasis.
- Stagnation of the product development process because there is no cross-project responsibility for continuous improvement.

Some activities apply to all product development projects and need to be properly managed across all of them. The PACE cross-project management element addresses some of these, including resource scheduling, business-systems interface, portfolio management, product development process engineering, and the interfaces into functional organizations.

The PACE Architecture

PACE is both a goal and a blueprint for the product development process. It defines product development as an integrated process in which individual activities, techniques, and tools work together within an overall framework. The PACE architecture can be viewed as seven interrelated elements. The elements of PACE and their interrelationships are depicted in Figure 4.

The first three elements (the Phase Review Process, Core Teams, and structured development) form the basic foundation of PACE. These elements are required for each product development project. The next four elements (product strategy, technology management, design techniques and automated tools, and cross-project management) provide the infrastructure for product development projects. They make it easier for these activities to succeed.

While the elements can be described separately, each is only truly effective within the framework of the total process. The success of any one element depends on others within the overall product development process. Core Teams, for example, can only be effective if they are truly empowered. Without the decision making that comes from the Phase Review Process, teams cannot be truly empowered, and their level of responsibility and authority becomes confused.

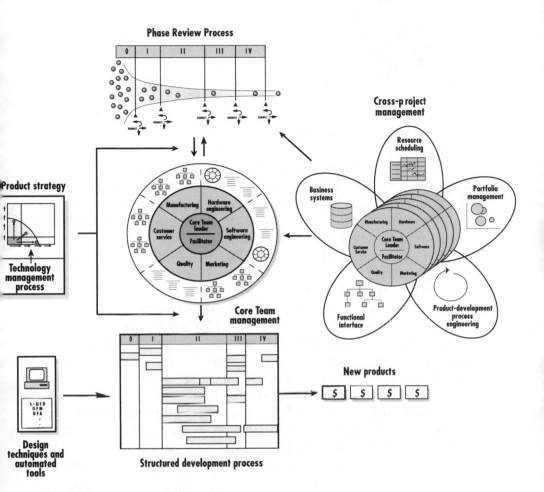

Figure 4. Overview of the PACE product-development process.

Likewise, if senior management makes the best possible decisions and the organization does not effectively implement them, new product development will fail. Core Teams or similar high-performance teams are essential to implement cross-functional requirements.

No matter how talented, a Core Team will take significantly longer to develop a product if it needs to reinvent the development steps involved for each new product. Therefore, a common structured-development process enables the Core Team to focus on developing a product, rather than on a process for developing a product.

Techniques such as QFD and DFM cannot be truly effective without a context in which to use them. QFD requires both a team to perform it and a process that emphasizes when it should be applied. DFM requires early involvement of manufacturing in product design, which in turn requires a team organization that makes it work.

Tools that automate the development process have proven to be less than effective if the process itself is not clearly defined. This is similar to manufacturing, where many companies invested heavily in automated equipment such as material handling and high-speed manufacturing systems, only to subsequently learn that just-in-time manufacturing and set-up time reduction eliminated the need for this investment. The message is the same: the process needs to be structured and simplified before automation can be truly effective.

Many companies have made reasonable improvements to this or that element of their overall development process only to be disappointed with the results. Piecemeal improvements often lead to increased frustration and a sense that "we've already tried that." There is no magic bullet. Dramatic improvement in new product development results from a wide range of improvements, large and small, that mutually support and reinforce one another.

PACE is not just theory. It is an approach proven by more than six years of successful implementation in more than 25 companies. Interviews by *Electronic Business* with companies that have implemented PACE demonstrate this.

- "This is the real stuff; this isn't theory," claims Michael P. LaVigna, president of Bolt, Beranek and Newman, a Cambridge, Massachusetts, manufacturer of computers, software, and communications equipment. "I can't imagine companies today doing product development without this process," he said, referring to the PACE process.[1]
- The Codex division of Motorola chopped its average product development time by 46%, while developing and shipping more products than at any other time in the company's history. In terms of quality, Richard P. Schroeder, formerly Corporate Quality Assurance Vice President, says that "new products have reached a sigma quality level of 5.5 to 5.7 (approximately ten defects per million operations)."[2]

- As a result of PACE, Whistler Corporation, a consumer-electronics company, introduced a new product in almost half the time it previously took. According to Charles A. Stott, Whistler's president, "An added benefit of the speed in development cycle has been a boost in product quality."[3]
- Until recently, Thomson Consumer Electronics' product development had never moved along very precisely. "We had modifications of the modifications," moans Erich A. Geiger, Executive Vice President of R&D.[4]

Summary

The only long-term sustainable source of product advantage is a superior product development process. PACE supports this by providing both a goal and a blueprint for a truly effective product development process.

- In PACE, new product decision making is implemented through a Phase Review Process that requires decisions at specifically defined milestones during development.
- The Core Team approach to project organization incorporates the best aspects of other approaches and overcomes their drawbacks.
- A structured development process ensures that a consistently improving process is leveraged by all development projects.
- Within PACE, product strategy provides the framework used by the PAC to make decisions and set priorities in the Phase Review Process.
- The technology management element within PACE focuses on the interrelationship of product development and technology.
- PACE enables the right design techniques and automated tools to be applied at the right time and within the context of an overall development process.
- Cross-project management addresses activities that need to be managed across all development projects.

References

1. Rick Whiting, "Product Development as a Process," *Electronic Business,* June 17, 1991, p. 32.

2. "Three Companies That Have Seen the Light of Product Development," *Electronic Business,* June 17, 1991, p. 68.
3. "Three Companies That Have Seen the Light of Product Development," *Electronic Business,* June 17, 1991, p. 66.
4. Barbara N. Berkman, "Thomson Fine-Tunes its HDTV Picture," *Electronic Business,* June 17, 1991, p. 85.

The Elements of PACE

3

The Phase Review Process and Effective Decision Making

Product development is driven by the decision-making process that determines what products to develop, and through this process senior management provides leadership and direction of product development. It sets priorities, allocates resources, and approves product objectives. Using this process, senior management implements product strategy and empowers project teams to develop new products.

Despite its importance, this decision process is often ineffective and may even slow down rather than drive development. Late decisions waste precious resources. Indecision causes projects to drift. Lack of consensus leads to frequent product changes. Scarce resources are overallocated, creating continuous delays and frustration.

Product development decision making is more than simply investing in any reasonably good idea with a return on investment above a targeted level. Most companies have ample new-product opportunities; selecting from among many possibilities is the real challenge. This requires executing product strategy through product development decisions.

New product decisions are interdependent; going ahead with one project takes away resources that could be used on another and opens up possibilities for subsequent products. Limited resources means that priority decisions need to be made among products, and even within a given new product, a choice needs to be made among alternative implementations.

In most cases the fault lies not with the capability of senior management but with the decision-making process itself—specifically, most companies do not have an effective decision-making process. Simply having a written policy or formal process is not enough; many companies that claim to have a Phase Review Process, for example, do not really follow it or have one that is ineffective. When this critical decision-making process is ineffective, people throughout the company conclude that senior management does not know how to lead product development. Frequently the real problem is the lack of a sufficient process for senior managers to do their job—an effective Phase Review Process.

Ineffective decision making is expensive. Our benchmarking shows that the estimated cost of wasted development because of poor decision making is surprisingly high.

The Phase Review Process is the element within the PACE process that enables effective product development decisions and drives the rest of the process. These decisions are made by senior management (referred to as the Product Approval Committee, or PAC) designated with the authority and responsibility for them. Phase reviews are decision-making sessions that occur at specific milestones in the product development process, and for each of these milestones there are clear expectations. Projects need to fulfill these expectations in order to continue.

The Role of Senior Management in Product Development

While everyone knows that senior management must be involved in product development, how do they actually do this? One executive shared his frustration in answering this question when he told us of the day he awoke with the desire to lead his company better in developing the best possible products. He arrived at his office that morning full of enthusiasm but didn't know where to start. He knew that leadership required more than solving problems related to completing products that were behind schedule. So he went to the lab and began to work with the engineers, giving them the benefit of his advice. He quickly realized that he was really not as capable as the engineers at the job they were doing. So he went to marketing and asked the people there what they saw as the opportunity for new products. Eventually he was so inundated with data that he got frustrated. At the end of the day he called for a status review by all project leaders.

At the review the next day he was briefed on all 14 active projects but had difficulty understanding any of them. The status reporting and formats were different. Too much status assessment relied on opinion, and all had excuses for why they were behind. They all asked that he get involved in resolving disputes among functional heads. At the end of the day, he threw up his hands, went home, and concluded that he didn't really know what his role should be in product development.

This case is all too common. Senior management may have the best intentions, but they frequently do not know what to do, when to do it, or how to do it.

Successful leaders clearly know what to do. We have found that there are several actions that they have in common.

1. *Establish the vision.* In some companies, senior management gets involved in the detailed product design, leaving the designers free to set the product strategy. The preferred role of senior management is to set the strategy by establishing the vision for their company's products. With a clear vision, the entire company can execute development activities to achieve it. Gordon Bell and Ken Olsen did this at Digital in the early 1970s with their vision of a common integrated architecture throughout the Vax product line. Jim Treybig did this at Tandem by establishing "the only's," the things that only Tandem's computers can do.

2. *Make decisions.* Today industry wastes hundreds of millions of dollars making product development decisions too late. Many companies decide to cancel or refocus a product development effort based on information that was actually known, or was knowable, much earlier. One large company, for example, estimated that it could save almost $40 million per year by making decisions earlier in the development process.

The reason for poor decision making is not incompetence. Usually, it is because there is not an effective process that enables senior management to do their job and make the necessary decisions. Senior management needs to review the right information at the right time to make the right decision. For example, a project team may present a complete design and even a model for a product, but the team has not yet determined the basic competitive differentiation. At this point it is almost impossible for senior management to conduct the necessary review to make the right decision.

3. *Cultivate the product development process.* A superior product development process can be a source of competitive advantage. While senior management cannot be involved in the details of all product development efforts, they can foster and cultivate the process for developing new products. This permits them to leverage their experience across all projects. They can invest in the product development process and set objectives for its continuous improvement. By supporting a common process, they smooth execution of product development activities.

4. *Motivate.* In some companies, product development teams go home every day at 5:05 P.M., while at other companies they are there all night if necessary. Some development people have little respect for their senior management, while others will make any personal sacrifice necessary. The difference frequently is how successful senior management is in motivating their development staff. Successful motivation and leadership in product development require that senior management has already achieved respect in the three previous roles. If management has not established a vision, if they cannot make good decisions, or if they do not understand the development process, then they cannot get the respect of the development staff that they intend to motivate.

Motivation is not a matter of technique. Specific motivational techniques depend on individual management styles and company culture. Senior management must recognize that motivation is part of their job.

5. *Recruit the best development staff.* Senior management can play an important role in recruiting the best product development staff. This is especially important when trying to attract someone with a unique technical skill or exceptional product development track record. To do this successfully, however, senior management must first understand what skills need to be added before they are needed. When management understands what is required, they can initiate and get involved in the recruiting efforts.

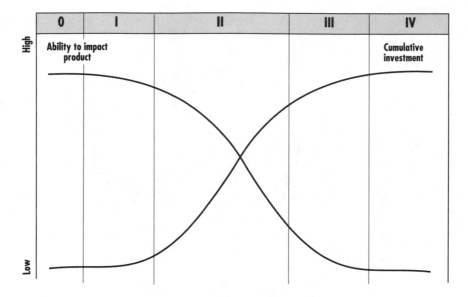

Figure 5. Management impact and resource involvement by phase.

Senior management also needs to know when to get involved. In our experience, senior management is most typically involved in new product development toward the end, when products are ready to be released. They get directly involved in fighting fires on products that are late or have problems. Unfortunately, by this time most of the decisions have been made and the real impact of their involvement is minimal.

Even worse, management involvement frequently slows problem resolution. The key individuals late in development are lower level engineers and technicians who can solve technical problems. Unfortunately, these are the people pulled away from their work to explain the problem to management, offer solutions, and wait for decisions.

The most effective time for senior management to be heavily involved in product development is up front, when strategic decisions are made and project direction is set. As the development project proceeds, resources are added and the work becomes progressively more detailed. Senior management's level of involvement should decrease accordingly as the ability to impact the product lessens. This is illustrated in Figure 5.

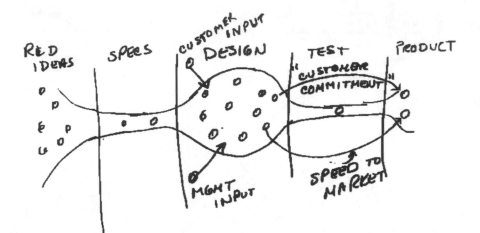

Figure 6. Company A's decision process.

Finally, senior executives need to know how to lead product development. This requires some sort of formal decision-making process.

How Decisions Are Typically Made

Many companies have not formally defined their decision-making process for new products. As a result, it is not clear when decisions need to be made, who has the authority to make them, how they are made, or what information is required to make them. This leaves everyone confused, and the product development process stumbles. This situation can be best illustrated with a couple of examples. As part of the training we do when implementing PACE, we ask groups of managers to draw a picture describing the way that new product decisions are made at their company. Figures 6 and 7 are representative of the way in which these processes are described to us.

The process for company A is described in Figure 6. It is pictured as a funnel, where the source of new products is R&D ideas. The product development flow is constrained during the specification phase and then expanded during the design phase. Customer and management inputs are not made until this phase, and obviously products tend to accumulate in the pipeline during this

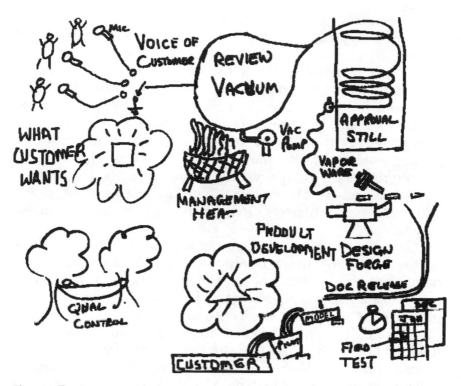

Figure 7. Company B's decision process.

phase. Very few products progress through the test phase, although customer commitments expedite products *around* this phase managers in this company jokingly refer to this expediting of products around testing and directly to the customer as their version of time to market.

Company B, shown in Figure 7, starts product development by listening to the voice of the customer. Unfortunately, the microphone is open to ground, thus losing the customer's inputs. What the customer wants (pictured as a square) is really just marketing's perception of the customer's needs. Projects then enter the concept review vacuum, where they sit waiting for management approval. Finally, in a panic, management turns up the heat and turns on the pump to force the project through a very small opening into the approval still. As the project sits on various senior managers' desks awaiting signatures, it is distilled. The product is then prematurely announced to customers with an aggressive ship date. This vaporware product is then driven by brute force through the design forge. Eventually, documents are released in a trickle to an overloaded manufacturing organization, which debugs the product on a model production line and then debugs the process on a pilot production line. By now chronically late, the project misses scheduled field tests. Quality control is doomed to fire fighting because it waited for the product to hit production before getting involved. Finally, the product ships to customers and, to the surprise of the company, underperforms in the marketplace, not only because of lateness but also because the resulting product (a triangle) was completely different from the initial requirement (a square).

During this process, time keeps passing, and the scheduled field test dates are missed. Quality control does not participate in development since it has better things to do. Eventually, document release trickles enough to build a model that evolves into a pilot product and finally into a customer product.

Although these illustrations are presented to be humorous, time and time again we see that there is no common view of, or respect for, the decision-making process. When 20 people from the same company are asked to describe their process, a listener would think they all worked in different companies. The jokes people make about their company's decision-making process show that they don't believe it works.

Cost of Late Decisions

Without an effective process, decisions to cancel or redirect projects are often made too late. What is the cost of these late decisions? While almost everyone experienced with product development intuitively understands that decisions should be made as early as possible, benchmark data have shown that early decision making is even more significant than most managers realize. Table I compares the cancellation pattern in one company to those of other companies considered to be the best in their industry. For purposes of simplicity in illustrating the differences in timing, we assume that in each case 100 projects are initiated, that the overall success rate is the same (48% of all projects started), and that the investment in each project is $1 million. The distribution

Table I Lost investment due to development-project cancellation at various phases (in thousands of dollars)

	Phase 0	Phase I	Phase II	Phase III	Phase IV	Total
Cumulative investment	$75	$175	$780	$920	$1,000	
Best companies						
Projects active	100	70	56	56	50	48
%canceled	30%	20%	0%	10%	5%	
No.canceled	30	14	0	5.6	2.5	
Lost invest ($000)	$2,250	$2,450	$0	$5,152	$2,520	$12,372
Total invest ($000)						$60,372
Case example						
Projects active	100	90	77	57	50	48
%canceled	10%	15%	25%	12.5%	5%	
No.canceled	10	13.5	19.1	7.2	2.5	
Lost invest ($000)	$750	$2,363	$14,918	$6,598	$2,510	$27,138
Total invest ($000)						$75,138

of the investment by phase is computed from benchmark studies for this industry.

Because of marketing analysis or strategic priority, the best companies cancel 30% of their projects after Phase 0, while the case-example company canceled only 10% at that stage. The total cost of these cancellations for the best companies compared to the case-example company was $2,250,000 versus $750,000. At the end of Phase I the best company cancellation rate was again higher—20% compared to 15%

But Phase II is generally where most of the development investment is made. At the end of this phase the best companies had no canceled projects, while the case-example company canceled 25% of its projects. The cost of these cancellations amounted to almost $15 million.

By the end of development, each company had successfully

completed 48 out of 100 projects originally started, with a total investment of $48 million for the successful projects. But the best companies only wrote off $12 million in canceled projects (20% of the $60 million total), while the case-example company wrote off $27 million (36% of the $75 million total). In other words, the best-practice companies developed 48 products at a cost of $60 million, while it cost the case-example company $75 million—25% more. At that rate, the best-practice companies would be able to develop 12 additional products for the same amount of money.

Product Approval Committee

In the PACE process, senior-management involvement is channeled through a formally designated product approval group. Typically this is referred to as the Product Approval Committee (PAC), although different names such as Product Review Board or new-product executive group may be used. In some cases it is the company's executive committee.

The PAC is designated within the company to approve and prioritize new product development investments. Specifically, it has the authority and responsibility to

- initiate new product development projects
- cancel and reprioritize projects
- ensure that products being developed fit the company's strategy
- allocate development resources

Because the PAC is a decision-making group it should remain small. Four to five executives is an appropriate size. It typically includes the CEO/COO/General Manager, Marketing VP, Engineering VP, VP of Finance, and Operations VP. Other senior executives may attend the phase reviews but do not maintain the direct responsibility for new product development. PAC responsibilities typically require 10–15% of a PAC member's time. This is a reasonable amount of time to spend in overseeing product development, and if the Phase Review Process is effective, it is an excellent use of time.

BBN Communications Corporation formed a product review board that consisted of the president and vice presidents of manufacturing, hardware and software development, and marketing. The product review board examined development projects at the conclusion of each phase and determined whether or not work should proceed. Ean Rankin, the division president, described the meetings as highly charged, with a tremendous amount of poking and prodding during the reviews because that is the time to find weaknesses in new products. The product review board made its decisions in a closed-door session and canceled several projects and redirected others. One of the major benefits of product review board and Phase Review Process at BBN was that management had greater confidence in the decisions it made.[1]

The Phase Review Process

The Phase Review Process drives the other product development processes within PACE. It is the process whereby senior management makes the difficult strategic-level product decisions, allocates resources to product development efforts, and provides direction and leadership to the project teams. These decisions are made through approval at the conclusion of specific phases in the development effort.

The Phase Review Process is intended to cover all significant product development efforts, including all major new product development opportunities. Also, projects that have a significant impact on multiple functional areas such as manufacturing, support, sales, and marketing should be included in this process. Very small projects such as minor enhancements are usually managed by a simpler process or grouped and managed as a package.

The Phase Review Process can be viewed as a funnel (Figure 8), with many ideas entering at concept phase and, through a series of screens over the course of development, narrowed to a few appropriately resourced projects with high likelihood of market success. At the conclusion of each phase of development, a phase review is held to determine the direction of the project: proceed, cancel, or redirect.

In Phase 0 a product concept is pulled together by a few people (usually a combination of marketing and engineering) in a short time. Since only a small amount of effort is invested, a company can afford to review many concepts, thus promoting creativity. During Phase I more people work on the project for 4–12 weeks to develop specifications and lay out a detailed development plan. With detailed planning completed, the PAC can now weed out projects that are not attractive enough or cannot be resourced sufficiently. Beyond the Phase I review the funnel should become

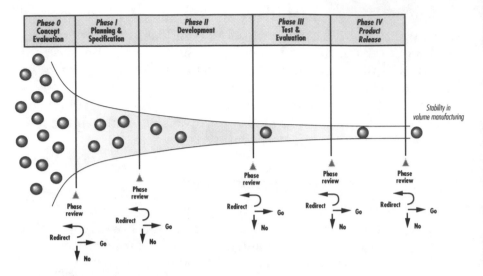

Figure 8. Phase review process funnel.

quite straight because significant resources will be committed to the project.

Phase reviews should be decision-oriented sessions and not briefings or presentations. The PAC should make a clear decision at the end of each review and communicate it clearly. This decision process should replace any procedures based on sign-offs.

At each phase review, actual performance is compared to plan. Critical product and project characteristics, are reviewed at each phase to assure performance and consistent direction:

- progress to schedule
- critical performance metrics
- projected product cost, margin, revenue, life-cycle cost
- development program budget and schedule
- important market, competition, and industry information

Under the PACE process, the project team (Core Team) is empowered by the PAC at each phase review to execute the plan for the next phase. As long as the Core Team stays within agreed-upon tolerances, the PAC does not need to be involved in details of managing the development effort. If major deviations occur during a phase, empowerment is automatically removed, and the Core Team leader is responsible for initiating an interim phase review to resolve the new situation. The Core Team is also responsible for devising a solution and for reviewing the proposed solution with the PAC.

The PAC approves funding for all resources on a phase-by-phase basis throughout the product development process. A project would not receive funding for the entire year but only for the next phase. A phase that covers multiple fiscal years would receive funding for the entire phase spanning those years. It is also necessary to take all authorized projects and relate them to the operating budgets and critical resources in a prioritized way so that the PAC knows how much can be allocated. If the funds or specific key resources are fully allocated, the PAC must prioritize project efforts to approve funding for the new project. The resource allocation process needs to be more clearly defined. This linkage is covered in Chapter 9 on cross-project management.

An effective Phase Review Process exhibits five major characteristics:

1. *Provide a clear and consistent process for making major decisions on new products and enhancements.* At the completion of each phase, the PAC determines whether the development efforts should be continued, canceled, or refocused; resolves major issues; changes resource allocation; and so on.
2. *Empower project teams to execute a project plan.* The Phase Review Process enables the PAC to set priorities, approve or revise project direction, set product and project goals, and monitor projects. It can then empower a project team to execute the next phase of the project.
3. *Provide the link for applying product strategy to product development.* Through the Phase Review Process, the PAC can direct development efforts toward overall company strategies.
4. *Provide measurable checkpoints to monitor progress.* The process defines the checkpoints that the PAC can use to review progress on both schedule and product objectives.
5. *Establish milestones that emphasize a sense of urgency.* Phase reviews are intentionally established as milestones where issues need to be resolved and decisions need to be made. These milestones instill a sense of urgency. A sense of urgency is necessary since most issues get resolved within two weeks of when they need to be resolved, no matter how much time is provided to do it.

Phase Requirements

The specific requirements of each phase vary by company, but we have found some commonality. In the first two phases, the requirements are related more to thorough planning and effective decision making. In later phases, there tends to be some variation based on the characteristics of the product being developed. A summary of the objectives of each phase, along with illustrations of the decisions at the end of the phases will help to make this clear.

Phase 0—Concept Evaluation

The objectives of Phase 0 are to enable a company to rapidly evaluate product opportunities and start the product development process as quickly as possible. A product opportunity usually enters this phase through the product strategy or innovation process. The result of Phase 0 is an evaluation of the concept and opportunity for the product, which is presented to the PAC for Phase I funding, and the outcome of a successful phase review is the assignment of a project team and funding for Phase I.

The primary focus of Phase 0 is to analyze the market opportunity and strategic fit. An example illustrates how this applies. A minicomputer manufacturer formed a team to design the second in a family of new products shortly after the initial product had been released. The team developed the concept for a higher-performance product incorporating additional features and new technology, but at the Phase 0 presentation they were unable to answer the question why this would be a winning product. The PAC sent them back to answer the question. After four weeks of intense work, where they contacted a large number of customers, they returned for another Phase 0 review with the answer to the question—a totally different product, a lower-cost version of the existing product that customers really wanted. Without the Phase Review Process the company would have spent almost $40 million developing the other product and would not have had the resources to develop the product that the market really needed.

An effective Phase 0 review can launch product development efforts in the right direction, even when it starts off in the wrong direction. This was the case when one company directed a small group to begin developing scaled-down versions of its existing products in order to open some new market opportunities. The team defined a new product incorporating the most essential features of a recently released product but at 80% of the cost. Although the team was quite enthusiastic about this product, the PAC realized at the Phase 0 review that this product would really just take away sales from the company's existing products and would not open any significant markets. As a result of this realization, they redirected the team to start again and investigate what would be required to open new market opportunities. Without this formal review point, the product would have been well on its way to development before these questions had been asked.

Phase 0 reviews can also pinpoint conflicting strategies between product development and other business functions. A signal distribution equipment company looked at a high-volume product recently with the objective of automating its manufacture. Upon investigation, it was determined that automation would reduce manufacturing labor cost from 80¢ to 55¢ on a product with a direct cost of about $9, yet not affect material costs that would yield much more savings. The investment in equipment was enormous, and operation and maintenance would be difficult in the developing country where the factory was located. Management finally confronted the real issue—it had a labor problem in the factory and thought it could solve it by automating the process and thus eliminating the troublesome workers. At the Phase 0 review the vice president of manufacturing was given the task of solving the labor problem on his own, and the project was redirected to look at the higher potential redesign focused on material cost reduction.

During Phase 0, a company evaluates an opportunity using assumptions—with the assumptions clearly identified and reviewed for reasonableness. This enables a company to take action before a significant investment is made. A communications company benefited from this when it launched a project to develop a product that would get it into a new emerging market segment. When the proposed product was reviewed in Phase 0, the PAC realized that the price of the product could be expected to decline below cost as the market emerged, and every unit would be sold at a loss. This was primarily because the new product lacked any unique differentiation from other products already in the market. The PAC canceled the project before significant development funds had been expended. Prior to the the new Phase Review Process, the company would have spent 18 months and $4 million developing the product and then not release it because it would lose money.

Only a few people work on the project during Phase 0. Generally this will include a product champion with the assistance of a few other key individuals. It is expected that the product champion will be encouraged to consult with other experts throughout the company in completing the phase requirements. If properly defined, this phase should be completed in four to eight weeks.

Phase I—Planning and Specification

Phase I is the fundamental building block of the product development effort. The objectives of this phase are to clearly define the product, identify competitive advantages, clarify functionality, determine the feasibility of development, verify to a greater degree of accuracy the estimates made in Phase 0, and plan the development effort for Phase II and the rest of the project. It is important that critical design elements are understood in enough detail to analyze their feasibility, but detailed design is not typically done in this phase. At the end of this phase, resource, schedule, and dollar estimates are made for the development of the product; however, funding will only be allocated to complete Phase II.

The Phase I review enables senior management to resolve any remaining issues necessary to make the product development effort successful. For example, the PAC at one company used the Phase I review to resolve some issues for a new high-volume electronic product with innovative performance characteristics. The PAC directed the team to focus more effort on the differentiating features of the product, assigned two additional software engineers in order to accelerate completion by two months, resolved the timing on the international release of the product, and initiated related efforts to improve the integration of this product with other products. Without a review point at which they had to be resolved, these issues would have stretched out indefinitely and slowed the completion of the product.

Phase I reviews also allow senior management to establish priorities between projects and allocate resources accordingly. A computer company launched an effort to develop a new disk storage device that was planned to require five engineers. At the Phase I review several interesting details came to light. First, the disk storage device could only work in conjunction with the next generation computer being developed, yet would beat the computer to market by over a year. Second, the project was now expected to require 18 engineers. These engineers would have to be taken off the next generation computer project, which would further delay its introduction. Finally, the new disk storage device would not be a dramatic improvement over the company's existing product already on the market. The PAC canceled the project and reassigned the engineers to higher priority programs.

Estimates of such factors as product cost, selling price, quality/reliability measures, projected unit sales, and completion date that were assumptions in Phase 0 are analyzed in more detail in Phase I. This was seen in a company developing a new product for a mature market. The product had more features and a lower cost than the company's existing products. During the Phase 0 review of the product, the PAC considered the cost assumptions to be too high and directed the team to focus on lowering them in Phase I. At the end of Phase I, the team recommended going ahead with the project even though the more accurate estimates showed an even higher cost. The PAC decided, however, that they did not want to invest money in a low-profit product for a mature market and canceled the project.

During Phase I, initial top-level designs may be started. For some product development efforts there may be a choice to be more aggressive and conduct more detailed design, but this should require specific approval at the Phase 0 review.

During Phase I more people are involved in the project effort, and at this point the project takes on the formal team structure such as a Core Team. Additional resources will also become involved in supporting the efforts at this time. At the end of Phase I, the PAC should decide either to cancel the project or to fund the Phase II effort, but it is also possible that the project team will be directed to resolve a specific issue before approval.

Phase II—Development

The objective of Phase II is to develop the product based on the development program approved at the Phase I review, and the majority of the detailed design and development activity takes place during this phase. Before beginning development, the company should conduct formal technical reviews of detailed specifications. During this phase the primary emphasis is on execution rather than analysis of the product opportunity or its feasibility

The company should initiate manufacturing and support-process development concurrently, including manufacturing and test-process development, product-announcement planning, and the customer-service process. Resource requirements significantly increase, and the majority of the development funding will be expended during this phase. Depending on the length of this phase there may be some periodic progress reporting, but if the project team encounters problems that significantly change any of the key factors, such as estimated cost or completion date, it should repeat the Phase I review.

Many milestones and intermediate completions occur during this phase, but the primary objective is usually the completion of a working product. The definition of *working* can be subjective in some cases, as one company found. At the end of Phase II the product, a high-performance computer, was working but not to expected performance levels. The PAC approved the release to Phase III with a modified approach that would work with selected beta-test customers to identify how to improve performance based on their use of the new system.

Approval from the PAC at the end of Phase II is the judgment that the product is ready for test and evaluation and that the plan for doing this is appropriate. In one project the PAC delayed approval at this stage because the software for the product was not sufficiently completed in order to do the necessary level of testing. The alternative, to initiate testing of the product with incomplete software, was proposed by the project team but rejected by the PAC.

Phase III—Test and Evaluation

The objective of Phase III is to complete acceptance testing and prepare for volume production and product launch. Completion of this phase is marked by a successfully tested product, approved manufacturing and support processes, and a product-launch plan.

At the completion of this phase, a Phase III review is held to make the final determination on whether the product is ready for initial shipment. Approval at this point is an approval to manufacture, market, distribute the product, and support it in the field.

One company with a strong commitment to quality uses this phase review as a final checkpoint to ensure that its quality standards are being met. In one Phase III review the PAC put the product on hold because it didn't meet quality standards and quality testing was incomplete. It did this even though customers were awaiting delivery of the new product. The PAC designated the vice president of quality with the authority to clear the release of the product when the standards were met.

Phase IV—Product Release

Phase IV typically includes volume production, product-launch marketing, initial distribution, and early support of the product. The Phase IV review is held to verify that these steps have been taken successfully. It serves as an assessment of early product performance and customer acceptance. Typically it takes place three to six months after initial shipment.

During Phase IV, the product is released to the market. Some remaining tasks may be associated with the initial release of the product, but they should be manageable in order to obtain approval. The remaining work does not include follow-on or enhancement efforts to software or other product options. At the end of this phase, responsibility is passed from the project team to the functional departments to manage the product on an ongoing basis. The project team, however, is responsible for resolving any product problems that occur before the Phase IV review.

The Phase IV review is also a convenient time to review product enhancement, general issues, and recommended process or design changes. For example, one company that launched a very successful product used this phase review to identify the opportunities to expand the product line based on early customer feedback. As a result, it launched two new projects into a Phase 0.

Summary

Product development is driven by the decision process on what products to develop. In this chapter we examined several key insights into this process including the following:

- Without specifically knowing what to do, when to do it, and how it should be done, senior management has difficulty leading product development.
- Ineffective leadership of product development has many impacts, such as confusion over decision making and development efforts wasted by late decisions.
- The key to successful leadership is an effective decision-making process, such as a Phase Review Process.
- Many Phase Review Processes are ineffective because they are poorly designed or not successfully implemented.
- In the PACE process, the Phase Review Process is the element that drives all product development activity.
- A Product Approval Committee (PAC) is the senior management group that clearly has the authority and responsibility to make decisions regarding new products.
- In a Phase Review Process, approvals are made by the PAC on a phase-by-phase basis, with funding and empowerment for the next phase.
- The requirements of each phase, particularly the early phases, are reasonably common, as illustrated by a detailed description of each phase.

Reference

1. Rick Whiting, "Managing Product Development from the Top," *Electronic Business,* June 17, 1991, p. 42.

4

The Core Team Approach to Project Organization

New products are developed through the coordinated efforts of many people. People who apply different skills and work together on many tasks, which, when completed, result in a new product. To work together successfully, they need to coordinate their activities, communicate what they are doing, and collectively make decisions. An effective project team organization is the key to making this happen.

Project organization and the way it works is one of the most essential elements of product development, yet few companies have implemented a consistently effective approach to it. Many do not even have a clearly stated way to organize product development projects; they leave it to each team to figure out how to organize. Not having a project organization is a little like selecting a number of people for a football team and then telling them to go out onto the field and play. The players do not know what position to play or how they should play together as a team. They may not even know who should be on the field when or who should do what. It is very difficult for a team to win with this type of confusion.

Other companies may be able to describe their approach, but it has not been consistently successful, usually because of organizational conflicts and an inconsistent understanding of how the team should work. Some companies experiment with different forms of project organization in hopes of ultimately finding the Holy Grail of product development. They attempt to improve product development by changing their approach to project organization each time a major crisis occurs.

What separates close-knit teams that work well together, rapidly bringing new products to market, from a gathering of functional representatives merely wasting time at weekly meetings? The close-knit teams are effective in communication, coordination, and decision making; these are the primary characteristics of successful teams. A variety of alternative approaches to project organization aim to achieve these characteristics, but these alternatives have generally fallen short of the high-performance level expected.

To overcome these shortcomings, PRTM developed the Core Team approach to project organization. It enables the quickest time to market through efficient coordination and communication, combined with effective decision making. The Core Team approach also provides the basis for true empowerment of the team and implementation of concurrent engineering of the activities involved in product development.

Characteristics of a Successful Project Team Organization

The secret to successful product development teams lies in organizing them to achieve effective communication, coordination, and decision making. Members of high-performance teams are able to effectively and efficiently communicate with each other without even realizing that they are doing so. Letting each other know about progress, issues, and key decisions is second nature. Many times this communication is transparent; it just happens as it is supposed to, enabling rapid execution and eliminating mistakes all too common in product development.

Coordinating the numerous activities that must be synchronized is also second nature to successful product development teams. Individual members know which activities must be handled carefully among other members and which can be handled on an individual basis. They know who has responsibility for various activities and when interdependency needs to be managed. Excellent teams are able to manage this coordination efficiently, without extensive meetings, memos, or other non-value-added administrative activities.

Effective decision making is the third characteristic of teams that excel in product development. As a team they know which decisions need to be made and when to make them. The team members understand which decisions are within their span of control and which require the attention of others with a more strategic or technical focus. They make decisions rather than letting things happen by default.

Communication

The high degree of uncertainty and variability involved in product development underscores the importance of good communication. Those working on the project together need to communicate results and identify issues that impact the work of others on the team. Problems need to be communicated to those who can help resolve them. Technical details and specifications need to be communicated to those who use them. Many questions need to be asked and responded to rapidly.

To be effective, communication must take place both vertically—without regard for levels or rank—and horizontally across functional boundaries. Communicating through a chain of command can be quite slow and error prone.

Much of the actual or true information can be lost through organizational filtering. For example, a managers may neglect to tell the full story to their director in order to give themselves some time to get the project back on track. The director in turn does more filtering prior to transferring the message to vice presidents, and so on. Soon all this filtering cleans the message to the point that senior managers think that everything on the project is going well. Eventually, they get surprised by an "unexpected" three-month schedule slippage. In reality, had effective communication been in place, senior managers might have been able to do something to help before the problem got out of hand.

Communication must be effective both vertically and horizontally in order to manage development time. Obviously, the more people involved, the more time is taken to communicate effectively. When communication requires repetition from one person to another, it is subject to delays. Project teams need seamless communication and access to executive management at critical points in the project.

Another reason to ensure quick and effective communication, horizontally across various functions as well as through the hierarchy, is to avoid mistakes in interpretation. The children's game of whispering a message to one person and having that person pass it on only to find out that the original message is completely distorted by the time it gets to the last person is played only too well by many companies involved in developing new products.

Finally, lack of communication has been the cause of many product deficiencies and project delays. The people who needed to communicate didn't. For example, on one project the project manager put together a schedule that assumed one week for tooling. Purchasing knew that a particular part required 12 weeks for tooling but never saw the schedule to estimate the tooling cycle time. Communication was assumed to have taken place but didn't. The product was almost four months late, and broken commitments led to lost customers.

The need for effective communication starts as the product concept evolves into a list of potential features and functions of the product. During this time, frequent, almost constant, communication is needed between marketing and development. Trade-off decisions regarding functionality, the partitioning of features, analysis of what competitors may do, the capabilities of the company, estimates of the market window, and the desires of the marketplace can be achieved only by effective communication within the project team. Rarely does a sequential hand-off from marketing to design engineering to manufacturing work successfully. The organizational structure of the development team can either facilitate easy and effective communication or make communication more difficult.

Some companies try to compensate by imposing extensive administrative communication. Development teams can get bogged down with these excessive non-value-added tasks such as preparing status updates, making management presentations, and coordinating formal approval sign-offs. One maker of industrial controllers, for example, had key technical people on the development team spending 30% of their time on activities that did not contribute to the successful completion of the project. These people were giving executive briefings twice a week, three presentations a week to other functions about the project, and conducting technical demonstrations about their great ideas.

So much time was spent on these tasks not directly related to completing the project that we estimated they could pull in their schedules by six months if they reduced this activity. Not believing this to be possible, we challenged one team to dedicate just one day a week to only developing the product. They could do no presentations, hold no meetings, or attend any management update sessions. They could only participate in design and development activity. The results from this minor change were so substantial that the team decided to reduce its nonproject activities even more, and as a result got its product to market in record time with a higher quality level than any other project in the company's history.

As the number of people on a given project increases, the number of possible communication paths rises almost geometrically. For example, a small project with only four individuals involved would have the following 12 communication paths for persons A, B, C, and D:

A→B	B→A	C→A	D→A
A→C	B→C	C→B	D→B
A→D	B→D	C→D	D→C

Product development commonly involves many more people, however. Figure 9 depicts the dramatic increase in communication paths $(N \times (N-1))$ as more people become involved in the project. With 60 people involved in product design, each issue or piece of

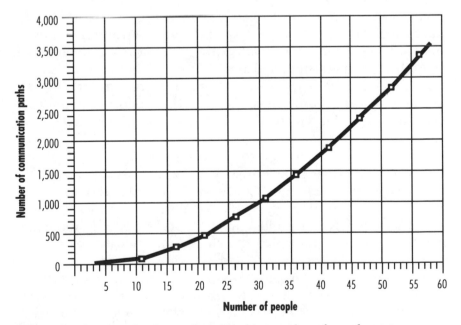

Figure 9. Communication paths related to number of people on a development team.

information can be communicated more than 3,500 ways, and when there are hundreds of these to be communicated each month, it can become quite complex.

Coordination of Activities

Developing new products requires the completion of thousands and sometimes hundreds of thousands of activities; many of these activities are interdependent. Efficient execution of numerous activities requires effective coordination, and as the complexity of the product or its marketing channels increases, the amount of coordination required to manage the project also increases.

Ineffective coordination can lead to project delays and inefficiencies. A multinational instrument company experienced this problem. Because the product development organization was convoluted, most of a project's time to market was spent in resource-coordination activities such as determining which technical experts should jump in to help the team at key points in the process, or backfilling for designers who were pulled to put out fires on other projects.

Ineffective coordination can also result in activities taking place out of sequence. All too frequently engineering begins development before marketing finalizes the product requirements. For example, a company designed and built working prototypes of the six printed circuit boards of a new computer only to find out that all had to be significantly changed when the product requirements were finalized. Eight man-years of key technical resources were wasted.

Some companies attempt to overcome coordination problems with comprehensive scheduling systems such as detailed PERT charts. Usually this requires significant overhead and does not effectively coordinate activities. One complex project tried to coordinate activities by using a PERT chart that covered a 30-foot wall. Two full-time people updated the chart continuously, but on any given day nobody knew what he or she was supposed to do.

Concurrent engineering involves effective coordination of all functions throughout a project, particularly in the early phases. This need for coordination has proved to be a roadblock for many companies that have tried to implement a concurrent engineering approach but can't seem to make it happen. Usually the reason is the inability of the project team organization to provide the coordination needed.

Successful project teams are able to efficiently coordinate activities with little wasted effort. They know what has to be done and who has to do it. Brief team meetings serve to coordinate upcoming activities, and they use the team organization structure rather than scheduling systems as the primary coordination process.

Decision Making

Developing a new product involves making thousands of decisions. Some are significant, many are small, but all need to be made efficiently. Making the right decisions on a timely basis is another factor that sets apart the successful from the unsuccessful project teams.

Effective project teams make better decisions. Different points of view, skills, and background provide them with synergy in decision making. We illustrate this during our workshops using an exercise called "Lost at Sea." In this exercise each individual is asked to rank 15 items that they would take with them if they were set adrift in the middle of the ocean. They then go through the same exercise in small groups. Each set of answers is then scored using U.S. Coast Guard rankings. Inevitably, the scores of the group are higher than the scores of the individuals, demonstrating the power of the team to make better decisions.

Product development decisions also need to be timely. When decisions go unmade for weeks or months, a project can drift and time to market lengthens. This has been one of the primary reasons for delays in product development. For example, one company developing a new product could not decide which microprocessor to use in its product. This was a difficult decision, but it went unresolved for almost 18 months. After six months, engineers began designing the product without the decision being made. When it was finally made, almost all the work needed to be redone and the product was a year late to market.

Empowerment of project teams is becoming a popular concept. In theory it gives the team the power to make the decisions that are needed. Unfortunately it is frequently stifled because the responsibility and authority of the project team are not clear.

Alternative Approaches to Project Organization

While there are many approaches to organizing product development, we find most companies have used a variation of seven general approaches: functional, customer/vendor, program coordinator, multiple functional project manager, project team by phase, matrix, or autonomous team. The functional approach is the most basic and also the most prevalent. To compensate for the failings of the functional approach, companies have either made their functional approach more rigid by adopting a customer/vendor model or tried to manage it better by assigning functional project managers. The matrix approach is an attempt to balance project and functional requirements. Autonomous teams simply pretend the rest of the company doesn't exist. Each of these tend to have some drawbacks; few companies are currently satisfied with their approach.

Some companies that do not have any clear philosophy for project team organization have evolved into using one of these approaches without a conscious decision over which was preferred. Unfortunately, when this happens, an organization results that has many different ways to develop a new product. It becomes difficult to see if product development is improving or not, and eventually the company ends up making the same mistakes over and over again.

The Functional Approach

The functional approach is perhaps the most prevalent organizational structure for development projects in the United States and Europe. Under this approach, each function contributes to the product development process in a serial, or hand-off, fashion—similar to a relay race. The development cycle starts with marketing's requirements for the product. These requirements are then handed off to engineering to prepare specifications and begin designing the product. Manufacturing then builds prototypes and pilot units, and sales next fills up the distribution pipeline. Finally, customer service gets involved to support initial sales and handle customer complaints.

The functional approach may lend itself to projects characterized by a defined series of sequences with minimal overlap, but it is generally not well suited to product development. We find that the functional product development approach tends to foster a "throw-it-over-the-wall" attitude, where people wash their hands of responsibility and accountability for the project once they complete their particular tasks. Many times this flaw is hidden because the organization is too busy to go back and compare the actual performance of the entire project to the original objectives.

Another drawback to a functional product development approach is that it usually creates a cumbersome system of sign-offs and approvals in which there are constant hand-offs *and* hand-backs. This time-consuming system typically arises from problems that occurred in the past. Once the problem is fixed, someone decides that avoiding it in the future requires a formal sign-off, where each function must review and approve the product before proceeding. That way there is an audit trail that can be reviewed in order to identify who is to blame. After a while the problems no longer occur, but layers of sign-offs have accumulated and development time has been extended.

For example, a manufacturer of electronic instruments overspent its prototype budget for materials by $860. Management countered by establishing a procedure that required four vice presidents to sign off on all prototype material procurement for a new product. The resulting time spent chasing these executives for their signatures greatly escalated development costs and needlessly lengthened time to market.

A functional structure has many vertical layers and generally lacks the horizontal network necessary for effective communication and coordination and rapid decision making that characterize successful product development. This can create functional gridlock, which stalls new product decisions. For example, if manufacturing does not order materials for a prototype unit until the designs are formally approved, structural delays creep in between the sequential steps. What starts out as a system with control points often becomes a bureaucratic maze that people circumvent instead of taking the time to fix. These are typical symptoms of companies that have longer product development cycles.

Figure 10 illustrates the confusing communication tangle of the functional organization approach. To develop new products under the functional approach, information must move horizontally across the various functions, as well as vertically through many levels in the organization. The number of communication paths quickly increases, and each communication path adds to total cycle time.

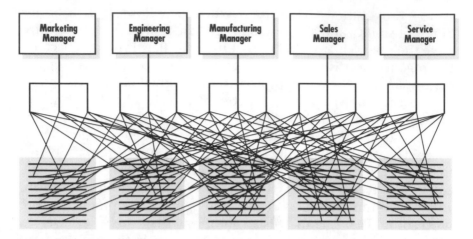

Figure 10. Functional organization, showing the interfunctional communication tangle.

When the functional approach works well, it is merely slow; when it works poorly, very few new products come out in time to be competitive. When conflict arises, issues get bumped up to the next level for resolution. Eventually, product decisions are made by those with the loudest voice or the most political clout, instead of the people closest to the design and the customer.

The primary defect of the functional approach lies in the structure itself. The performance of people within any given function is measured and rewarded according to that function's goals and objectives. As a result, those involved in product development tend to strive for functional excellence. Often what is best for the individual functional organization, however, may not be good for the product or company as a whole. Functional goals may not always be consistent with company goals, and they are frequently inconsistent with the goals of other functions.

Project teams at a minicomputer company were functionally organized with marketing and sales, R&D, engineering, advanced manufacturing, manufacturing, and customer service. Each of these functions was involved in the new product development process at different points in the process. Marketing usually initiated development with a list of requirements that it thought a new product should have. Marketing passed a marketing requirements document (MRD) to the engineering organization. Engineering consequently would start with the MRD and decide what it would and would not do. A product functional specification (PFS) would then described what engineering would design. Unfortunately, the marketing requirements document and product functional specification were typically not aligned.

Manufacturing became involved in the project only when it came time to build pilot units. Since the engineers ordered all the parts and built their own prototypes, manufacturing had to start from scratch. Much time was spent trying to understand the design and to find standard, acceptable components. Finally, just before the first customer shipment, customer service found out about the project. Of course, it needed to have spare parts strategically located around the country. This meant that manufacturing had to ramp up even faster and that engineers had to stabilize the growing number of engineering changes quickly.

As a result of this functional orientation, the company took twice as long to develop new products as its competitors. Eventually it was sold to a foreign company, which attempted to make improvements only to be frustrated by the strong functional mentality.

While individuals within disparate functions often know their profession well, they may not understand what is important to other functional groups. Figure 11 illustrates that what one functional expert finds rewarding and interesting frequently has no bearing on the interests of experts from other functions. Each step that one works on individually is shaded by one's own specialized interests. This bias shapes the product in ways that detract from its success.

At a computer manufacturer, marketing specified that a new

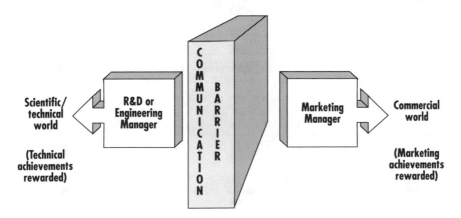

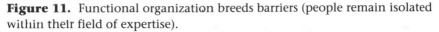

Figure 11. Functional organization breeds barriers (people remain isolated within their field of expertise).

computer should be able to meet all the needs of a wide variety of industry and military applications. Engineering added the specification that it have the most advanced processor technology that would be available in a year. Although these extremes were not necessary, the product was defined to include them. After a year, the company realized that the product would cost so much and take so long that it was redefined to focus on real needs.

The functional organization structure for product development works well in small, closely knit companies with limited product variability. In these firms, everyone knows everyone else and generally they all have ample experience working together. Start-up companies exemplify this and are frequently used as models for how this approach works. Where a small company is developing a single product, however, the entire company is essentially a project team.

The Customer/Vendor Approach

The internal customer/vendor project structure is an extreme form of the functional approach that seeks to achieve functional integration through formal documents. With this approach, each functional organization acts even more independently (see Figure 12), contracting out its services to the other organizations in the company. Transactions are conducted formally with many approval stages along the way.

In customer/vendor development organizations, the process occurs as follows:

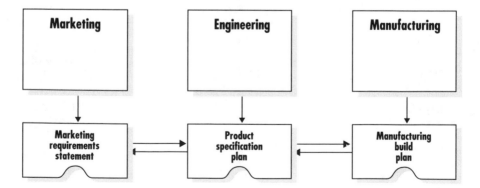

Figure 12. Internal customer/vendor organization.

1. Marketing sees a need for a new product and creates a marketing requirements document, which it submits to the engineering department for response.
2. Engineering reviews the marketing requirements document and evaluates technical feasibility and resource availability. The engineering department responds with a product specification, as well as estimates of time, development expense, and rough-cut product cost.
3. The two organizations go through a period of negotiation, trade-off discussions, and a formal sign-off approval cycle before the actual work can begin.
4. Once the product-approval cycle is complete, engineering then breaks the product into modules and writes contracts for different groups to deliver these modules. Once again the negotiation and sign-off process begins.
5. Once the design is well under way, the engineering department contracts with the manufacturing organization to develop production tooling, order prototype and pilot materials, and design manufacturing processes.

The customer/vendor approach inherently introduces delays into the product development process. All communication is through formal documents, which require longer periods of time to prepare. These documents tend to become more and more detailed as past omissions and miscommunications result in disputes. The response and acceptance process requires many iterations. In some cases we have seen these iterations appear to continue indefinitely since product requirements change as the disputes go on.

Most products are too complex to use formal hand-offs as the only means of communication. This results in omissions and misinterpretation, which lead to problems later in development. Since many of the best product designs result from the interaction of those with different skills, this approach frequently results in less successful products.

This process creates an extensive audit trail of documents to formally support individual positions. In one case marketing had written a memo saying that the two versions of a new product had to be released within a month of each other. The software plan indicated that the programming effort would require almost a year between the two versions. Neither read the other's documents, and both assumed that because they issued a written order it would be followed. By the time the difference was realized it was too late to make the trade-offs that were necessary.

Another company in the advanced materials business followed the internal customer/vendor approach of project organization. The company was so functionally oriented that even the functional heads reported primarily to a corporate functional officer, which resulted in only dotted-line ties to a given business. Every step in the development process required extensive documentation and sign-offs for each hand-off of the development effort. Up to 11 signatures were required for these hand-offs, and most projects had 14–16 major hand-off points.

Product development people in this company were quite frustrated with this process. They would work late at night and sometimes all week-end to get a sign-off document completed for management. Management typically took 6–12 weeks to concur on the document and sign it since it had to go to corporate functional management for review. This resulted in huge gaps with little or no activity on each project. Projects took so long that many times the market changed enough to make the original product idea inadequate. This meant that the project team had to begin the process all over again. This company began to lose market share to more timely competitors and eventually decided to change its approach to project organization.

We experienced the most extreme example of the customer/vendor approach in a small company making high-performance computers. Issues would be stated in detached, departmental terms: "Marketing expects these features to be inclusive in the design." A typical response from design engineering would be: "Engineering does not believe these features are important and shall not consider them." This company was trapped in a functional stovepipe so deep that it lost sight of what customers wanted in its products. Each function was seeking to grow in size and power yet was adding no value to boost sales and increase the customer base.

Program Coordinator Approach

Another variation of the functional approach is to assign a program coordinator to manage schedules and coordinate activities. This approach has its roots in defense contractors, where this was a required function—hence the typical reference to program rather than project.

Frequently the people in this position are referred to as program managers or the department of program management. They are rarely involved in any actual management, however, nor have they been given the authority to do so. Their primary role is to prepare schedules, usually assigned to them out of a frustration that there are no overall project schedules. Sometimes the schedules are prepared with the integrated input from those working on the project, but all too frequently they are not believed by the people actually doing the work.

In its worst form, program coordinators revert to a watchdog role. They independently audit the progress of projects and report problems to senior management.

At best, program coordinators are Band-Aids to problems in the development organization. There is no change in the organization itself, there is merely a coordinating mechanism put in place to compensate for some of the deficiencies in this approach.

One company typified this evolution. The Office of Program Management was established to provide schedules for projects that were using the functional development approach. This was necessary since no one had the single responsibility for the project. Pulling together a real schedule proved to be difficult since the functional schedules were inconsistent and uncoordinated. So the Office of Program Management prepared its own schedule, but nobody used it except senior management. Nonetheless, the office grew to a staff of more than 35, while at the same time became perceived by the development staff as the company's internal spy network. Clearly, the office provided very little value to the company, and the money would have been better spent on developing product.

The Multiple Functional Project Manager Approach

With the multiple functional project manager approach, each function has a project manager (see Figure 13) so there are many project managers and teams at the same time. The idea behind having a product development project manager from each function was to shore up some of the weaknesses of the

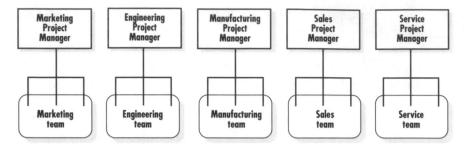

Figure 13. Organization showing multiple functional project managers.

functional approach by having someone manage each of the major function's responsibilities. Each of these project managers manages the project throughout the development cycle, although each one generally has more influence when his or her function is most involved.

A major data communications manufacturer used this organizational structure in the late 1980s in an attempt to capture the benefits of functional excellence and matrix management. When problems arose, however, the system began to break down, and finger pointing between each functional manager was rampant, each claiming that others upstream or downstream dropped the ball. The company abandoned this approach after only 11 months. Little value-added work had been done, and the company's major product development effort had been stifled.

A major shortcoming of this structure is lack of overall accountability when problems arise. Each project manager can point fingers upstream and down to lay blame. Furthermore with each manager attempting to optimize his or her own function, this almost always results in suboptimization of the project as a whole.

The Project Team-by-Phase Approach

Another form of project organization is project team-by-phase. Under this structure (see Figure 14), a different team is responsible for each phase of the project. At the completion of each phase, the project is handed off to a different team for the next downstream phase.

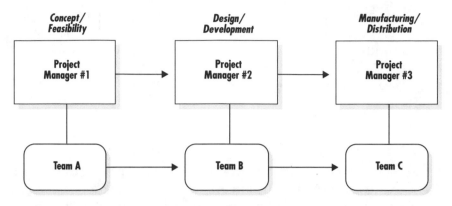

Figure 14. Project manager/team-by-phase structure.

This approach seeks to take advantage of specialized skills in each phase. It assumes that individuals will perform better if they focus on a piece of the development process rather than the entire development cycle.

In a study we conducted on best practices, we did identify a disk-drive manufacturer with unique requirements that was quite successful using the team-by-phase approach. Design engineering worked closely with customers but was geographically separated from manufacturing. It completely excluded all other functions from the design process and worked exclusively with the customer. It even went to the extent of restricting other functions from visiting its facility.

When a new disk drive was completed, design engineering passed the design and prototype to the domestic manufacturing facility, where it was redesigned to be more manufacturable in low volume. Later, domestic manufacturing passed it to the Asian manufacturing facility that redesigned it for high-volume manufacturing.

The company had the fastest time to market in its industry. It optimized the design time by working directly with the customer that specified the product. Manufacturing developed a skill in redesign. This success, however, appears to be unique to the characteristics of the advanced technology module designed to a specific customer specification and then manufactured in high volume.

The project team-by-phase structure tends to degenerate when the development process accelerates, because much time is needed to communicate activities between teams, particularly at hand-off points. Another difficulty is tracing accountability once problems arise. If each team has not documented all of its activities in detail, addressing problems becomes time consuming and complex.

The Matrix Management Approach

Some companies have organized product development teams along the matrix management approach popularized in the 1970s. Matrix management attempts to break down functional walls. The basic philosophy underlying matrix management has people within a given function "loaned out" on a full-time or part-time basis to work on a specific project (see Table II). The matrix model attempts to take the best from the functional organization and combine it with a temporary project focus. It has had some success but requires a significant amount of executive time to ensure that the project team is managed fairly. Often the matrix organization lacks effectiveness because of the pressures of political influence within the company.

Matrix management requires clear goals and objectives for each project, project managers who are well respected, functional managers and project managers who can communicate freely and often on an individual's performance, and executive managers who have the time and are willing to continuously monitor progress. Without clear goals and objectives for everyone involved, matrix management breaks down. Every individual must be reviewed continually in terms of goals and objectives for the project and the function. Because product development is such a dynamic activity, typically goals and objectives have to be set and reset several times in the course of a year. Failing to do so means that the individual being evaluated has no chance of being successful for both the functional and project responsibilities.

Under the matrix structure, project managers must be well respected. There is much less emphasis on the team's performance as a group. Therefore, for a project to succeed, project managers must be very strong in their ability to get things done without alienating individuals in a structure that does not give them direct authority.

Table II. The matrix management approach

	Project A	Project B	Project C	Project D	Project E
Marketing Manager	X			X	
* * *					
Electronics Engineer	X	X			
Electronics Engineer				X	
* * *					
Software Engineer				X	
Software Engineer	X	X			X
* * *					
Manufacturing Engineer	X		X		

The matrix structure also depends upon open communication between functional managers and project managers. How often does this truly happen? Typically, since the roles of project and functional managers are in somewhat of a conflict, there is mistrust and consequently poor communications between the two.

The last, and perhaps the most difficult, element of matrix management is that it requires a great deal of executive management time and discipline to monitor and control. In reality, this type of discipline is difficult to consistently apply because of the time requirements of keeping the individuals involved satisfied with decision making.

Matrix management usually fails because an individual's responsibilities and loyalties are in constant conflict. Essentially, team members operating within this structure must satisfy two masters: the project manager and the functional manager. Usually whoever has greater influence over performance evaluations wins out. Matrix management tears individuals between doing the right thing and satisfying their performance objectives for the function. Project ownership becomes even more difficult if a person is being matrixed to two or more projects.

For example, if an industrial designer is working on four projects and has several functional responsibilities during the same period, much of his or her time will be spent on attempting to manage priorities in order to satisfy everyone's objectives. Eventually, this person does whatever he or she can instead of doing what is best for the projects and the company as a whole.

True matrix organizations are rare. More typically engineers work on specific projects where there is no input into their annual performance evaluation. On paper that may look like a matrix structure, but in reality development personnel have more of an allegiance to their functional management, with little accountability to the success of the project. Our experience with the matrix organization for product development shows that when critical issues or conflicts arise, the decisions made are based not on what is best for the company but on who wields the most power, the project manager or the functional manager.

Autonomous Teams

Perhaps the most extreme approach to project team organization occurs when the team is given absolute autonomy. The various colorful names for this approach include skunk works, swat team, and tiger team. Some of the most dramatic product development successes have been achieved with this approach. The Eagle project described in the best-selling book *The Soul of a New Machine* [1] applied aspects of autonomous teams.

In this approach, the team is given a general sense of direction, provided with the necessary funding, separated from the rest of the organization, and left alone to develop a new product. Team members make all their own decisions and develop the product they want. Generally, they are only accountable by delivering a successful product.

Start-up companies and new ventures follow essentially the same model. The management is funded by investors based on a business plan, and the entire company functions as a product development team. It is a streamlined organization with a single focus: developing a new product. Organizationally the structure is simple. The CEO is the team leader and the functional vice presidents are responsible for the development activities in their areas. Most importantly, the skill level of this company-team is generally much higher than an equivalent team in a larger organization with many projects under development.

However efficient this autonomous team approach is, it has two fatal flaws. The first is the total dependence on the project team. Since there are no checks and balances, the decisions and judgments of the team are final. The team needs to have all the experience and technical skills required. This includes the management experience in the process of product development. The failure of many start-up companies can be traced to this weakness, leading many venture capitalists to conclude that the three most important characteristics in a new investment are management, management, management.

The second fatal flaw is the impact that a completely autonomous team has on overall company strategy. Since the team is completely autonomous, it doesn't take advantage of the skills and experience throughout the company. It doesn't link into the company's customer base or core technology. Additionally, the autonomous team can stifle the achievement of other company objectives such as design for manufacturability, concurrent engineering, or a coherent product strategy. A manufacturer of high performance systems used this approach and cut development time in half. Unfortunately manufacturing yields were only 40% due to tight design margins, and a poor understanding of manufacturing methods.

Autonomous teams have their place, such as new ventures with solid management or diversification projects, but they are not a cure for all product development ills. One company fell into this trap by putting a new team of bright developers in an off-site location with an unlimited budget and a vague direction to develop the next generation of products. A year later the developers were still studying the possibilities, and senior management dissolved the project.

Valuable lessons can be learned, however, in some of the characteristics of the autonomous team. If the focus, efficiency, and motivation could somehow be integrated with the company as a whole, all objectives could be achieved. This is the philosophy behind the core team approach.

The Core Team Approach

When we first started working with our clients to improve the product development process, we developed the Core Team approach as an alternative for organizing product development teams. After applying the Core Team concept repeatedly with exceptional results, we realized that it was a superior way of organizing, directing, and managing project teams. We now believe that it is the best form of project organization for product development.

While the Core Team generally consists of five to eight individuals with different skills and a Core Team leader, it does not use the classical hierarchical approach to organization. All product development responsibilities are divided among the team members, and individual team members' responsibilities are usually associated with their skills. Recognizing the need to move away from vertical hierarchies, strict functional representation, and pay-grade level politics, we believed that the Core Team structure had to be represented by a continuous circle. As the circle implies, all team members are equals. No single function has more status than another.

The circle also suggests that everyone faces the same challenge: to do what it takes to get the right product out to the customer quickly. This implies completing tasks that may be outside team members' strict functional areas or below what would normally be considered their stature.

Individual team members focus less on representing a function and more on carrying out the tasks that contribute to the ultimate success of the project. They do not operate within the normal constraints of job descriptions; they are more flexible and work as a team to do what needs to be done. Core Team members execute their responsibilities directly, on their own, by supervising people assigned to them and by coordinating with functional specialists.

The Core Team approach differs from other forms of project organization in that responsibility lies directly with the Core Team and not with the functional organization. In the functional organization, responsibility is imposed, while with the Core Team structure, accountability is accepted. In a hierarchical structure, detailed decisions are generally made or approved at higher organizational levels, but in the Core Team organization decisions are made closest to the point of action, by the people most familiar

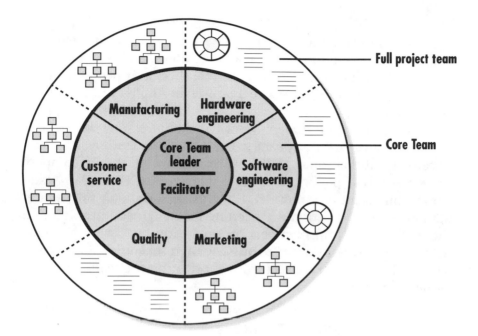

Figure 15. Basic Core Team structure.

with the problem. To help them make the best decisions, Core Teams can get advice, counsel, and guidance from functional specialists.

A Core Team organization consists of four main elements: a Core Team leader, the Core Team, the full project team, and the Core Team facilitator. These are illustrated in Figure 15.

Core Team Leader

At the center of the Core Team is the Core Team leader. This individual has the responsibility and accountability for ensuring that the product meets its goals for quality, schedule, and cost. The Core Team leader is the hub that drives the team. The role of a Core Team leader varies in a subtle but significant way from that of a project manager in a matrix organization. The Core Team leader is more of a team captain than part-time boss. The emphasis is on leadership, not dictatorship. This person acts as the quarterback (in the American football analogy), leading and motivating the team to achieve the design and project goals.

The Core Team leader is also responsible for managing the budget, resources, and schedule. The Core Team leader works to resolve conflicts among Core Team members, and when conflicts or issues arise between Core Team members and people in functional organizations, the Core Team leader helps to bring about resolution.

Good Core Team leaders do not make unreasonable demands on their team. On the contrary, the best Core Team leaders have excellent interpersonal skills. A telecommunications company once made an experienced product manager the Core Team leader for an important new product, but this person didn't fully understand the role. He constantly alienated the engineering and manufacturing Core Team members by pounding his fist on the table and screaming that they were missing their schedules and budgets. This had the opposite effect from motivating the team to get the project on track.

Core Team Members

The Core Team members surround the Core Team leader. The specific makeup of the Core Team will vary based on the product being developed, its complexity, and its market. For smaller, simpler projects, the Core Team could consist of as few as four or five people. In contrast, very complex projects with hundreds of people involved in the full project team could have as many as ten people on the Core Team. In any case, a Core Team should almost always include members from engineering, manufacturing, marketing, and customer service.

Core Team members coordinate project activities for their particular functions. They act as conduits (see Figure 16) for communicating both functional needs into the development effort and project requirements back into the functional organization. This ensures a product that is manufacturable, serviceable, and meets customer requirements.

Core Team members also manage the project resources for the activities that they have responsibility for. For example, the electronic engineering Core Team member in a data communications development team manages engineers working on processor, communication, and interface boards, as well as those working on

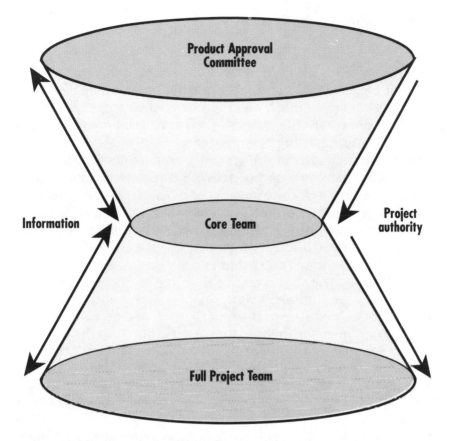

Figure 16. Core Team as information conduit.

backplanes and the power systems. These individuals are members of the full project team. Members of the full project team work on the product at specific points in the process. Full project team members come into and exit the project as their work is completed. The responsible Core Team members contribute to the performance evaluation of their full project team members.

One U.S. consumer electronics company no longer has a quality function represented on the Core Team. This company has achieved so much in the way of improving quality that it is an integral part of every person's job. Quality needs no representation because it is already imbedded in the team.

Full Project Team

The next layer out from the Core Team, the full project team comprises the individual contributors from various functions that are involved in a portion of the project managed by a specific Core Team member. Members of the full project team can be assigned directly to the project or are functional managers who are involved in supporting new products.

Those assigned directly are typically product development engineers, technicians, and specialists who complete various project tasks. For example, ten software engineers can be assigned to software development. Full project team members can be assigned permanently or temporarily, and full-time or part-time. Their work is coordinated by the Core Team member they are assigned to.

Functional managers and other experts may participate as part of the full team. They are typically involved in coordinating specific activities. For example, a component engineer and purchasing manager may be involved in the qualification of a new supplier.

Core Team members frequently have members on the full project team who are not resident in their own functional organization. For example, a hardware Core Team member often has full project team members from CAD, regulatory, component engineering, procurement, and manufacturing engineering functional organizations.

Full project team members work on the project either full-time or part-time, depending on the scope and intensity of their work. They typically come into the project when needed. It is the responsibility of the Core Team member to negotiate with various functional managers for the time needed. Core Team members typically will provide input to the performance evaluations of individuals working on their full project teams.

Facilitators

Facilitators are charged with helping the Core Team leader and members through the development process. They have a process improvement focus versus a project focus. Many people think of them as an on-line help system to guide the Core Team through the steps in the development process and through initial phase reviews.

Project facilitators help the Core Team utilize the product development process to achieve the most possible. They are process engineers who understand how to get things done. They also frequently assist the Core Team leader in planning, scheduling, and coordinating project activities.

Additionally, facilitators measure the development process, monitor trends, plan improvements, implement new tools, and so on. Their responsibility is to be the manager of the product development process and assist in implementing it across all projects.

Functional Managers

At first many functional managers are uncomfortable with the implementation of the Core Team structure in the organization. They question their own role in an organization where the Core Team will make all project-level decisions.

In reality, it is impossible for functional managers to participate in more than one or two simple projects and still maintain their functional responsibilities. Some try to implement elaborate progress reporting; others use weekly briefings. While this may help them to understand the process, it does not enable them to contribute to the project's progress. The result is excessive overhead, built-in decision-making delays, and confusion over who is responsible.

The Core Team structure works to free up functional management by getting them out of the day-to-day, implementation-level details of product development. By doing so, functional managers can then concentrate on functional excellence, advance the technical knowledge of their organization, set long-term plans and strategy, and allocate resources across multiple Core Teams. They therefore not only become more efficient but they also better leverage their experience.

Under the Core Team structure the role of the functional manager changes substantially. Instead of getting bogged down in day-to-day implementation-level decisions on specific projects, functional managers set the strategic direction for their function, provide the source of technical excellence to their people, staff and support Core Teams, and measure and improve their portion of the new product development process.

For a functional manager, moving to the Core Team structure

can be somewhat threatening. It's not very comfortable knowing that your people, who in the past came to you with every decision, will now be making implementation-level decisions on their own or with their fellow Core Team members. Typically this requires a transition period, since individuals will be new to the Core Team member role and not confident in their ability to make decisions, and functional managers usually need to see a track record of successful decision making before they are willing to relinquish some control.

Time to Market and Project Organization

Figure 17 illustrates how time to market is directly affected by the way a project team is organized. On the horizontal axis is the approach to resource participation that ranges from staff assigned task responsibility regardless of the project to resources dedicated to a project team. The amount of coordination and communication required to develop the product is also plotted horizontally, on the lower horizontal axis. Generally, less coordination and communication is required as project participation moves toward more dedicated resources.

On the vertical axis, project management approaches range from essentially no management to a single project manager who is in charge from start to finish, with many variations in between. Also on the vertical axis is the time required for decision making. This goes from slow to rapid as more-focused project management greatly reduces the amount of time required to make decisions.

Seven forms of project organization, including Core Teams, are positioned on this chart to illustrate the performance differences of the various approaches. Those positioned up and to the right have more efficient coordination and communication as well as efficient decision making. The Core Team and autonomous team organizations have the highest performance, but the autonomous team is so extreme that it sacrifices any functional involvement.

A company making telecommunications products was able to increase project effectiveness by changing its approach to project organization. Traditionally, it had specific functional task teams or experts that participated in subelements of a given product's design. These subelements were optimized by each task team; however, no one took an overall product viewpoint. The company spent weeks making the simplest of decision because many people participated in the project, each having his or her own view of what was right. Coordination was done by a large staff function called project administration. It was this group's charter to attempt to coordinate a high level of activity across many individuals. Communication went up vertically in the functional organization, then horizontally across functions, and then down vertically again.

Dedicating project resources for major projects and selecting a single project manager from specification through to volume manufacturing acceptance helped to greatly reduce this company's time to market. Projects that had taken 50 months in the past now took 30 months to complete. Decisions were more timely. Coordination and communication became more efficient. By making these improvements the company was able to move from the lower left-hand sector of the chart in Figure 17 to the upper right-hand sector. They moved along the diagonal that improves time to market.

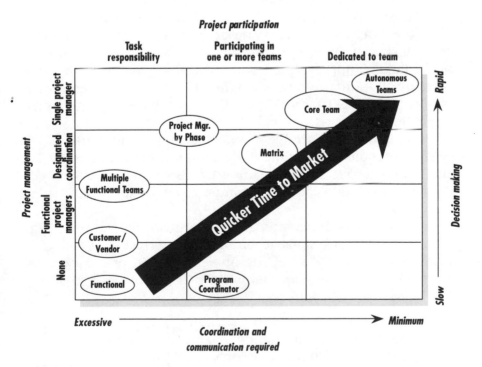

Figure 17. Time to market and project organization.

Empowerment

Empowerment involves giving a group the responsibility and authority to do a specific job. It is a powerful concept, but it is often misapplied. One product development consultant claimed that the true test of empowerment is "when a project team can develop any product they want and they are not restricted by company policies requiring approval for things like hiring, capital spending, etc." This is the wrong interpretation of empowerment.

Meeting common goals and objectives is easily facilitated by giving Core Team members the authority and accountability for the project's success. This authority and accountability come from empowering the Core Team with finite, measurable milestones of performance and the resources for development.

PACE enables effective empowerment by establishing a two-layer organization with executive management (as the Product Approval Committee) and the people directly involved in developing a new product (the Core Team). For nonproject issues, Core Team members report to and are evaluated by their functional managers. For specific product development, Core Team members are evaluated by the Core Team leader, who in turn is evaluated by the Product Approval Committee. The PAC empowers the Core Team by allocating resources for the project at each phase of the project. This gives the Core Team the authority for all implementation-level decisions.

By empowering Core Teams to make implementation-level decisions in product development, decision making becomes quicker and more effective. Everyone understands who makes what decisions, *and* these decisions get communicated to those who need to know.

With the Core Team approach, senior management makes the critical strategic decisions regarding the product, but the Core Team members make all of the implementation or tactical decisions necessary to develop the product. This provides two important benefits to the company:

1. Executive time is spent providing strategic direction and control instead of micromanaging lower-level decisions or arguments between functional departments.

2. Most of the project-related decisions are made by the Core Team, which is closest to the project. Because they live and breathe the project every day, these people have the necessary information to make decisions.

The benefits of Core Team empowerment became clear to a vice president of a major computer company who loved to make every major product decision for his 300-person organization. Managers were constantly hounding him, however, to make important development decisions. Once the company established the Core Team structure, this vice president was freed up to focus on the future growth and direction of engineering. Equally important, people developing products learned again how to make good development decisions.

Implementing Concurrent Engineering

Concurrent engineering means developing the product and all of its associated processes, that is, manufacturing, service, distribution, at the same time. The Core Team structure allows a company to *implement* concurrent engineering. It brings the proper functions into the development project at the correct time. With the Core Team in place, companies develop not only the product but its associated manufacturing, distribution, and service and support processes as well. The objective is to have everything in place before the product hits the market. By dealing with process considerations during design, time to market is generally shorter. Concurrent engineering typically also produces the benefit of lowering overall product cost because manufacturing and other processes are optimized.

A Department of Defense technology assessment team reviewing Japanese technology-based companies found that concurrent engineering allowed companies such as NEC, Toshiba, and Sony to greatly reduce time to market and lower total product life-cycle costs. The team also found that concurrent engineering implemented through organizational structures like the Core Team resulted in higher-quality, more reliable products than those from U.S. and European competitors not employing these techniques. Consequently, these companies also have more efficient resource utilization and a greater rate of revenue per employee than their competition.

By using the Core Team organization structure to implement concurrent engineering, companies can begin to break the project revision cycle (see Figure 18). The project revision cycle starts with problems occurring during the project. Of course, many of these problems could be avoided or managed better if the Core Team approach were used to implement concurrent engineering. These problems, usually in the crisis stage, result in changes in the project. Sometimes the scope or functionality of first release has to be changed; sometimes changing the team members or leader is needed. Altering the project in these ways leads to longer development cycles as people regroup and begin to replan and restructure their efforts.

The vicious part of the cycle occurs when as a result of longer development time, the market shifts towards another approach and the company must struggle valiantly just to catch up. An even worse scenario occurs if a paradigm shift in technology takes place. (This can be a "bet the company" situation.)

One manufacturer of thermally activated power switches lost the project revision cycle game. The firm was so caught up changing to its new product under development that its projected completion date slipped first three months, then six months, then finally an entire year. In the meantime, a competitor was working on a new switch technology that cost one-tenth that of the technology used in the current product. The competitors got to market first and the project revision cycle company had to permanently close its doors, eliminating 260 jobs.

By implementing the Core Team structure and allowing concurrent engineering to really take hold, a company can induce the functions to become stronger as they focus on what they can contribute to new product development. Their task is not to optimize their functional department for the purposes of creating an empire but to staff properly and support ongoing operations as well as product development.

Figure 19, which is based on a survey we conducted, illustrates when best-practice companies involve the various functions in product development and to what degree. On the vertical axis, various functional organizations and groups involved in new product development are listed. Across the top of the chart, major steps in the process from concept to volume manufacturing stabil-

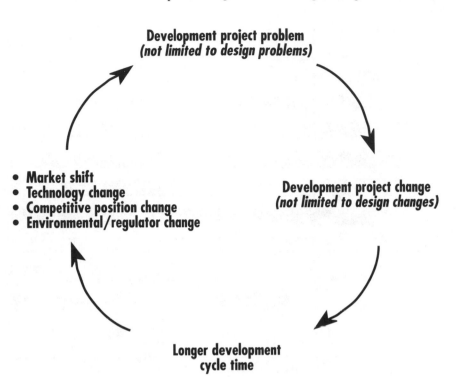

Figure 18. The project revision cycle.

ity are shown. The shading indicates the level of involvement each function has at the various points in the process.

Research is involved heavily up front to transfer technology from the lab then transitioning to a monitoring mode. Engineering is involved heavily throughout development, including the hand-off to manufacturing. Manufacturing has substantial involvement early in development, thus designing manufacturability instead of scrambling late in development. Marketing does not just kick off development but is involved throughout to handle trade-off decisions and prepare for market introduction. Sales is kept informed of the upcoming product and gets involved during testing for sales training and preparation for launch. Quality plays an active role throughout for both product and process design. Service is involved moderately so that serviceability issues are addressed. Finance monitors development throughout to assure the

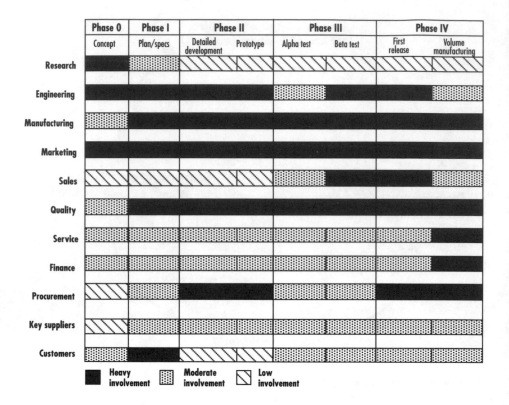

Figure 19. Concurrent engineering integrates all functions during the development process.

project is financially justified and on track in terms of budget. Procurement and key suppliers are involved from specification onward so that all parts and subassemblies can be easily integrated and fully utilized. Finally, the product's concept and specifications are validated with customers as well as test units.

Summary

Companies following old paradigms for project organization simply won't be able to competitively develop products in the 1990s. The reasons for this are as follows:

- Effective communication, coordination, and decision making are essential characteristics of successful project teams.
- The seven traditional forms of project organization have not been consistently successful in achieving these characteristics.
- The Core Team approach is a new, more effective paradigm for project organization.
- The Core Team includes a Core Team leader, Core Team members, a full project team, a project facilitator, and a different relationship with functional managers.
- Successful project team organization can improve time to market.
- The Core Team approach enables teams to be effectively empowered.
- The Core Team organization structure implements concurrent engineering.

References

1. Tracy Kidder, *The Soul of a New Machine* (Little, Brown, Boston, 1981).

5

Structured Product Development

In many companies, the way products are developed is completely unstructured. There is no consistent terminology; each project team uniquely defines its activities, even though many are similar. As a result, project schedules are not comparable—some define 20 activities while others define 1,000 activities. There is no way to compare progress across projects, and standard cycle-time estimates cannot be used for scheduling. Without a common structure, the product development process cannot be improved easily.

By *structured* we mean having a framework with terms describing what's done in development, which is consistently applied across all projects. Because all projects have some things in common, some elements of structure should be the same for all projects. Because projects vary in their complexity, timing, and ambitiousness, some elements should vary with these factors. Because some aspects of a project are unique, some elements should be left to the team to define.

Structuring the activities of product development is a key element of PACE. It includes defining these activities so that everyone clearly understands what has to be done, how it is done, and when it is done. With a structured process in place, the emphasis can be on rapid execution.

Because technical experts, engineers, and managers think of product development as an art, they resist structure. *Structure* to some may wrongly imply stifling control or bureaucracy.

Structured product development in PACE strikes a balance between discipline and creativity. A well thought-out process doesn't hinder creativity; it allows it to focus on the real issue—

developing the product itself—not in reinventing *how* to develop the product each time.

Structure in development doesn't stifle innovation as long as it isn't extended too far. In PACE, development activities are seen as grouped in a hierarchy, from *phases* (the highest or broadest level) to *steps* and *tasks* to *activities* (the most specific). Phases are the same for all projects; activities are left to Core Teams to specify. The intermediate steps are the same for all projects (although some projects may omit some). Tasks may vary by class of projects. Collectively, they form the basis for project scheduling, resource planning, process measurement, and continuous improvement.

The Need for Structure in the Development Process

Because many companies don't think of new product development as a process, they have never defined the activities required to develop a new product. Even basic terminology is undefined. For example, each project includes a functional-description document, what that document includes should be clear to everyone. It should not be thought of as a ten-page summary by one engineer, a 60-page document by another, and a 400-page document by a third.

Lack of consistent terminology wastes enormous time and effort as those using a vague process try to make sense of it. Typically, extensive and unproductive meetings may be needed just to understand what is going on. Much of this wasted time is due to the lack of structure.

In one case, a data communications company without a structured process seemed to have twice the development resources it required for the amount of development activity under way. Upon investigation, we found that only 30% of people's time was actually spent on designing the product. The other 70% was wasted clearing up misconceptions about what was being done and by whom. Terminology was so inconsistent that product specifications had four different names and twice as many definitions.

Over the past six years we've surveyed hundreds of people involved in product development at many companies spanning a broad range of industry. We inquired how they could benefit by structuring their development process. The results are quite interesting:

1. Hand-offs between groups are misunderstood and often fumbled:

   - Fully 39% of the hand-offs received are garbled or confused, causing wasted effort, misdirected work, and so on. This means that if a project has three hand-offs, at least one is guaranteed to be messed up. Since most projects involve many hand-offs, this problem is huge.
   - Interestingly 22% of work is *knowingly* passed on garbled or confused. The many reasons for this include inadequate planning, rushed execution, and lax discipline.

   While this is disturbing enough, 39% of work is *received* garbled or confused. How did the level increase from 22% to 39% (a 17% discrepancy, which is almost double the original 22% level) in the transition? The relationships are fundamentally misunderstood between different groups in the development process. In other words, downstream groups' needs are not understood or appreciated by upstream groups. For example, the CAD group may not know what specific information and format that manufacturing needs for the bill of materials and thus messes up the hand-off.

2. Fully 42% of work is repeated because of an upstream change such as late customer input, specifications in error, or something was overlooked. This means that two out of every five working days are wasted! If repeat work were eliminated, the productivity of the development organization would increase by 72% (58% good work to 100% good work) without adding any people!

3. At least 48% of development work is fire fighting—unplanned work that pops up unexpectedly and must be dealt with immediately. Fire fighting solutions are primarily Band-Aid solutions due to time-pressures, limited resources, and limited alternatives because much of the design is already locked in. Fire fighting work is hastily done and usually fraught with errors.

4. A full 48% of plans created by individuals involved in development are questioned, ignored, or otherwise discredited by managers or peer groups. Since product development is an inherently complex and multifunction process, the overall project schedule is based on the integration of many lower level schedules. Yet one out of every two schedules is rejected.

   Why is this so? Probably because early schedules are only 45% accurate! Since the early schedules are inaccurate, no one believes them. Management then issues unreasonable demands, and the development team responds by padding the schedule. Eventually all schedules become smoke and mirrors, and product development becomes a crisis.

5. Amazingly, only 28% of development work is truly new. This means 72% of the work is familiar. If this is so, then why do the problems just described occur? Because there is no process structure and learnings are not captured. Structuring the development process focuses on the 72% of work that has been done before—the mundane blocking and tackling that so often bog down projects. With this work structured, development teams can focus their energies on the 28% of work that is truly new and innovative, which subsequently adds the most value.

These survey results show the tremendous opportunity that structuring the development process presents.

Concerns Regarding Development Process Structure

Innovation and creativity cannot be precisely planned and controlled, but structuring the routine activities makes possible a focus on the more creative aspects of product development. Traditionally there have been some concerns regarding structuring the development process in technology-driven organizations. Many people treat product development as a creative process. Indeed, portions of product development require some creativity.

Based on PRTM's extensive client data base, however, this is typically 28% of the project. Once creative people understand that structure, at the appropriate levels, can actually free them of the mundane and boring tasks, they will have more time to spend on the creative, value-added elements. For example, rather than take time to determine the outline and format of a functional specification, engineers can better use their time applying a standard format and defining the product.

Many people feel that structure confines. They complain that it's too rigid and limits flexibility. We agree. The wrong level of structure results in extensive paperwork and bureaucracy. Finding the right level of structure for the type of product is important.

When working initially with a client, we sometimes hear that "structured development processes won't work here because we never do the same type of project twice." This is almost never true. Even widely disparate projects have much in common.

Moreover, if product development is approached differently each time, two things happen. First, there is no repeatable learning-curve benefit, so cycle times gradually get longer as projects grow more ambitious. Second, when someone does come up with an improved method or technique, it is not standardized and leveraged by other projects. If steps in the development process are not approached in the same manner each time, it is very difficult to measure the process and improve it.

Many technical people are uncomfortable with structure. They worry about being confined and losing flexibility and creativity. Yet when product development activities are truly understood, it's easy to see that most of them are not new. In fact, PRTM's experience with technology-based product development has shown that for most new products, most activities are not truly new. By structuring the repetitive tasks and activities, technical experts become freer to concentrate on what is truly new and unique.

For example, one company in the advanced systems market had a senior technical person who refused to believe that product development could ever be structured. When probed about the new design she was working on, she initially said it was "all new." Upon further investigation, we discovered that, in a hardware sense, only two of the 56 circuit boards were new. Then, after looking closely at each of these, she determined that only four ASICs (application specific integrated circuits) and some supporting logic was new.

Still another company designing early warning systems for major defense contractors fell into the trap of using its wide product variety and low production volume as excuses for cost overruns and missed schedules. The company believed that this cycle couldn't be reversed because each project was different. Once it understood that although projects may be different, they have common process elements, the company was able to structure its process to be more competitive.

Symptoms of the Need for More Structure

Indications that a company needs more structure in its product development process can be seen in many ways.

Inconsistent terminology and definitions

Every company has its own product development language. Unfortunately, all too often this language is similar to the tower of Babel—everyone speaks in a different way, assuming that everyone else understands it in the same way. With terminology that is inconsistent from project to project, people don't understand the context and scope of what has to be done. One company had ten different names for the same market-assessment document. Each version was slightly different, but those differences became more blurred over time. Eventually, no one was certain what the document was supposed to contain. This confusion leads to much non-value-added activity devoted to understanding what people truly mean when they use a term or say they are going to complete a task.

Inaccurate schedules

Product development schedules are only as good as the accuracy of the steps that make them up. If the steps are not clearly understood, then it is difficult to estimate how long they will take. If they are inconsistently defined, then it is impossible to use past experience as a reference point. Inaccurate schedules frequently result from an unstructured process because people are scheduling on assumptions that may not be shared or understood by others in the organization. Nonexistent schedules are an extreme version of inaccurate schedules.

Inability to estimate resource requirements

Resource requirement estimates are only as accurate as estimates of the time taken to complete each step. Without a good consistent definition of each step, it is impossible to make reasonable estimates. When the estimates are inaccurate, companies are continually late with new products and projects are under- or over-resourced. Structure helps by first defining what has to be done and how long it will take. Once this is understood, the ability to accurately estimate resource requirements greatly improves.

Plans made disjointedly between groups

Without structure, there is little basis to make critical decisions. Plans made by one functional organization don't tie into what other organizations are doing. This results in key activities falling through the cracks. In an electronic systems company that suffered from lack of structure, there was no consistent framework, terminology, or definitions. Consequently, management frequently got lost in the details. Each project manager presented different formats, processes, and levels of detail. Executive managers often weren't able to see the forest for the trees. They grasped onto points that were not important and had to make decisions with an unclear picture of how it all tied together. Without structure, coordinating plans made between groups is virtually impossible, since everyone has a different understanding of what must happen.

Excessive task interdependence

Excessive task interdependence occurs when tasks in the development process are delayed or waiting in queue for another task to be completed. An unstructured or poorly structured process is full of this sort of wasted time. Clarifying process tasks and defining what is required for each one greatly reduces task interdependence. Failure to clarify the process leads to waiting on nickels, where low-cost activities slow down or hold up high-cost activities.

Poor understanding of responsibilities

Poor structure results in not knowing who or what group is responsible for the completion of specific activities. PRTM often works in organizations where the responsibility for critical tasks is not well understood. We have seen fully staffed departments where no one else in the organization knows exactly what the department is doing. This is a key indicator that the development process is confused and roles and responsibilities for the activities are not clearly defined.

Attention focused on fire fighting

Excessive fire fighting is symptomatic in companies with insufficient product development structure. A computer company we worked with was stuck with a fire-fighting dilemma where executive managers loved to jump in, roll up their sleeves, and help solve problems. They were more comfortable jumping from crisis to crisis than in setting strategy and objectives for everyone else. This came to a head when the executives asked a project team to give them two one-hour updates every day at 8:00 A.M. and again at 5:00 P.M. The team, of course, spent an hour preparing for each status update and lost four hours of productive work time every day.

No "one way" of developing a product

A company in the electronic imaging business had no consistency from project to project. The steps followed to develop a new product occurred at different places and times for each project. Many of the activities had varying nomenclature, making it difficult for people who had worked many years in the division to interpret what was happening. As a result, no one took advantage of good methods when they were developed.

Too many clarification meetings

Poor process structure leads to a multitude of meetings for clarification purposes. Because next steps are vague, these meetings are required to figure out what has been accomplished, what must be worked on next, and who is to do it. Too many meetings is a sign of a poor process structure.

Large middle-management ranks

The need for structuring new product development is clearly evident when management has to make decisions. Understanding how each project fits in the overall product line plan, its integration with the R&D or technology strategy, and its financial justification can be greatly simplified by a structured process. Without structure, more middle management is required to handle the confusion. Companies that have the correct level of structure have fewer middle management people, as they are not needed for controlling the process.

Time wasted on non-value-added activities

Extensive non-value-added activity can be incurred to clarify terminology and intent. The magnitude of this can be enormous. Without structure, more time is spent coordinating activity and redoing tasks because of miscommunication.

A systems company that structured its development process eliminated the white spaces in the process. (White space is time spent during which no value is being added to the project.) This company consequently cut 23% off the cycle time for new products. According to the vice president of engineering, "The real value of this was that we can now use that time and those resources elsewhere, giving us the freedom to work on more new products."

How Much Is Enough?

Companies typically are at either end of the spectrum when it comes to structuring new product development (see Figure 20). In unstructured companies, the activity levels in the development organizations are quite frenetic. Everyone is extremely busy; no one has time to think, and people really can't see how their pieces of a project fit into the bigger picture. Typically in these companies, little is written down, and senior management has to spend most of its time fighting project-related fires.

In contrast, companies that are too structured typically have two systems in place. The first is represented by the five-pound development notebook on everyone's shelf that management thinks is being used. The second is the true process that people follow because the five-pound process is too bureaucratic and slow. These organizations may have done some excellent work in defining the product development process, but typically few projects actually follow the overstructured guidelines.

The correct level of structure balances the need for a repeat-

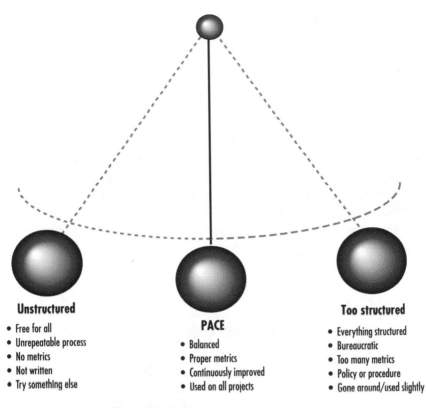

Unstructured

- Free for all
- Unrepeatable process
- No metrics
- Not written
- Try something else

PACE

- Balanced
- Proper metrics
- Continuously improved
- Used on all projects

Too structured

- Everything structured
- Bureaucratic
- Too many metrics
- Policy or procedure
- Gone around/used slightly

Figure 20. Range of process structure.

able, measurable process with the requirement to remain flexible and open to new ideas or approaches. By providing structure at the proper level and time in the development process, PACE focuses on achieving this balance so the development process is used, measured properly, and continually improved.

Levels of Structured Development

Structured product development is a hierarchical blueprint of the product development process that is consistently applied to all product development projects. Within PACE are four levels of structured development; each level is an aggregate summary of the previous level.

Hierarchical Structure

Structured development under PACE consists of four hierarchical levels: phases, steps, tasks, and activities. Figure 21 graphically depicts these levels. As can be seen in this chart, there are typically three to six phases, multiple steps within phases, multiple tasks in each step, and multiple activities in each task.

At the highest level of structure are phases. As described in Chapter 3, there are usually three to six phases. Phase end points are milestones in the development process where decisions are required for funding of the next phase. Each phase consists of a number of specific steps.

Steps are the most significant level within structured devel-

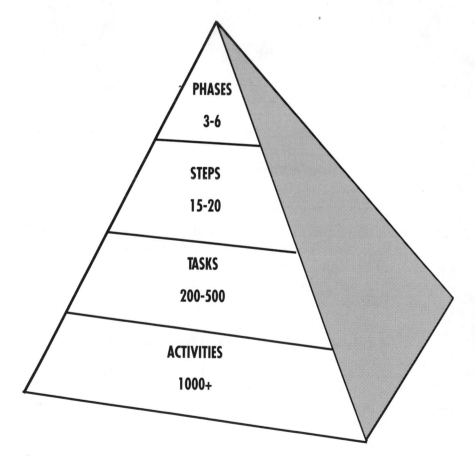

Figure 21. Levels of structure.

opment. These are used to schedule and manage the progress of development activities. Most companies have 15–20 steps in their development process. Steps are consistently applied to all projects, although some projects may not include all the steps. A software-development step, for example, would be the same in all projects, but projects without any software development would omit that step.

Steps consist of multiple tasks—typically 12–35 tasks for each step. Generally, tasks are consistent from project to project unless there is a significant reason to change them. Tasks are used to compute standard cycle times and define the work to be done. Task completion is the responsibility of the Core Team member in charge of a specific step.

Tasks are broken into a number of activities. These activities can number from several to more than a hundred per task. They are the things that every project team member is doing on a day-to-day basis. Unlike tasks, activities tend to vary based on individual projects since the actual work may be divided differently from project to project.

Project Overview

Structuring the development process at a high level starts by creating a one-page overview of the entire development process, from concept to volume manufacturing. This high-level overview outlines the phases of development, defines the major steps in the development process, and shows the parallelism, precedence, and overlap of the various steps.

Under PACE the steps in product development are defined as part of a generic structured development process. Figure 22 shows an example of a typical generic process. The generic development process for a particular company will vary somewhat depending on the type of product being developed, markets into which the product is sold, product uniqueness from a technical and marketing perspective, product complexity, organizational structure, and culture in place.

The generic structure is used to define a specific project overview for each project. Project overviews clearly delineate the major steps of product development and the phase-review points at the end of each phase. At this time steps are specifically estimated and schedule dates are added to the overview.

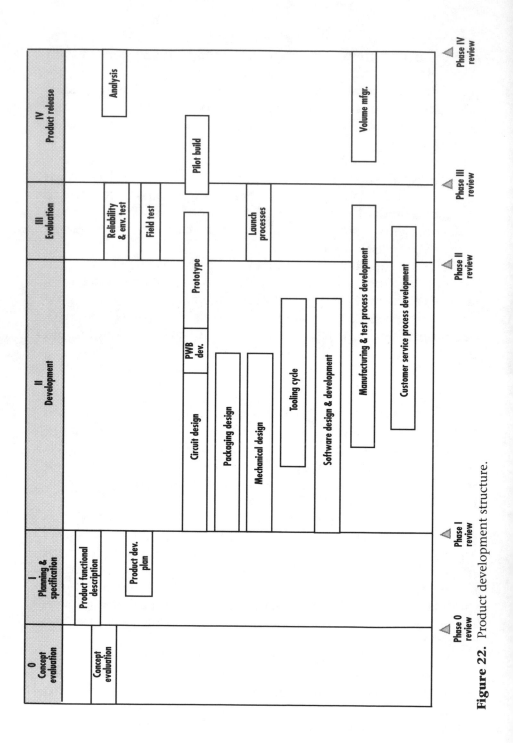

Figure 22. Product development structure.

The entire company should see and understand this high-level, one-page overview. It becomes the vision for the project. If the project cannot be simply laid out on one page, then it cannot be clearly understood by those doing or managing it. From executive management to first-year designer, everyone should know the steps in the process and how they all fit together.

Steps

Steps are the most critical level within a structured process. They are the basis of scheduling and provide the link between phases and detailed tasks and activities. Our experience defining steps in a structured development process tell us that it is critical that they be defined properly.

If steps are not properly defined, then a company will be unable to achieve a significant improvement in time to market. The definition of the process itself could constrain product development activity by requiring excessive non-value-added activity, stifling concurrent engineering and teamwork, or sequencing activity inefficiently.

One company, for example, asked an experienced engineer to define the steps in its product development process. When he completed the definition, the company's CEO directed that everyone in the company follow them. Although his intent was to reduce time to market, because the steps were not properly defined, time to market actually increased.

The steps in a structured development process should be clearly defined and consistently applied. Take the functional specification step, for example. Everyone should know what the functional specification includes, how comprehensive it is, how long it takes to develop, and when it is scheduled in the design process. It becomes common terminology, and the emphasis can be on execution. Steps define the deliverables expected during or at the end of the step as well as the review points, such as design reviews, that are part of that step.

Steps should be consistently applied to all product development projects. Product specifications, for example, should be done at the specified time in the schedule, with the same scope and to the same level of detail from project to project. Senior management can then rely on the specification being done and understand what it includes.

Tasks and Activities

Each step consists of a number of tasks that define more specifically how that step is done. The flow of tasks not only defines what needs to be done but outlines the sequence as well. Figure 23 shows a sample flow of tasks for a typical software design step. This begins with a task to review software requirements developed in a previous step and goes through the tasks required to complete and review the software design.

The task level within structured software development also defines how the development is to be done. The software design example implements a structured software development approach by defining that high-level design be done and reviewed before module design. Module design and review are then performed. The example also shows that the proper planning for testing be done simultaneously rather than when coding is complete. As a result, the company can implement a more disciplined approach to

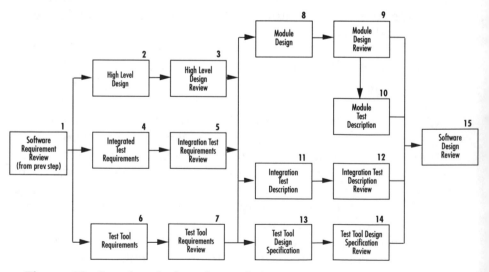

Figure 23. Sample tasks for software design step.

product development where the design is completed and reviewed before coding.

Detailed Development Guidelines

The focus on "how to" is important in order to leverage the product development learning experience. For example, a manufacturer of discrete semiconductors had detailed guidelines of what was to be done, but only the most experienced development managers knew how to do it. This company's growth was limited by the amount of senior-management time available to help people learn the process. Consequently, senior managers spent all their time in development instead of running the business.

Guidelines for the development process provide many benefits to an organization, including

- capturing learning across multiple projects
- increasing proactive up-front thinking as opposed to fire fighting
- establishing a starting point for process measurement and improvement
- enabling scheduling based on what the process is capable of producing, instead of speculation about process capabilities

The intent of process guidelines is to capture the present knowledge that exists in people's heads or in filing cabinets. If each project uses guidelines for implementation, people quickly begin to find better ways of conducting product development. These improvements can then be reflected in continuous updates of the guidelines so every project can leverage new methods. Guidelines help capture this learning on an ongoing basis.

At the start of a development effort, the Core Team should use the latest version of the guidelines as an aid in planning the project. Each team member should review his or her respective guidelines and identify any potential problems or high-risk areas. These can then be reflected in the team's development plan.

A company must carefully consider the type of guidelines and level of detail required before guideline creation. Development guidelines can range from simple one-page flowcharts and checklists to detailed descriptions of critical activities. The style and depth will depend on the company's culture, complexity of products, and markets.

The test for all guidelines is a simple one: they must be readily adopted and easily used by development teams. If every project is not using the guidelines, then the guidelines must be changed because people will eventually circumvent them. When all projects use the guidelines, problems and bottlenecks with the current methodology can be quickly identified. Addressing these problems one by one will assist an organization to become world class in new product development.

Scheduling with Structured Development

Few people would challenge the importance of creating a schedule for product development work and managing activity to such a schedule, but most people don't like schedules or understand how to successfully create one that works. A good schedule is critical to reaching the market window on time. It becomes the focus of control and a means of communicating progress to the entire project team.

Scheduling product development is difficult for several reasons. First, many details about the development are undetermined. Many companies, however, try pushing a development team to commit to an end date before the team has even completed the design specification. Once the team commits, even if it has laid out all of its assumptions, management tends to lock in on a crude estimated date and can't understand why later, when the project scope is better defined, the estimated date no longer holds. We frequently hear management stating to teams that "you haven't even started and already you're eight weeks late."

Scheduling is also difficult because resources are not always available when the team really needs them. Typically, time is lost waiting for the right people or tools to become available.

Finally, most people are too optimistic when asked can you do this by such and such a date? It's not that people are inherently dishonest, it's just that many of us don't schedule with correct capacities in mind. If, for instance, a normal work week is 50 hours for a development professional, then to do a schedule based on a 50 hour per week availability is unrealistic because it does not take into account vacation, sick time, training, administrative tasks, and assisting on other projects. These activities must be accounted for, leaving remaining time as that which is available for new work.

Three-Level Scheduling

Product development has become so complex that the standard approach of one person creating, managing, and controlling a development project plan no longer holds. Techniques such as critical path method (CPM) and project evaluation review technique (PERT) are inadequate for product development. Development is essentially an information flow; a physical entity is often not realized until the prototype-build stage. Because techniques such as PERT and CPM were created primarily for physical flows, they are insufficient for managing product development successfully.

PRTM has developed the three-level scheduling technique specifically for product development. It uses structured development as the basis for developing and managing schedules.

Product development calls for dissemination of information at many levels. Three-level scheduling enables varying levels of project-management detail for different audiences. Managing the inappropriate level of detail frequently results in either poor decision making or micromanagement of the design team. Recognizing this problem, we have given three-level scheduling multiple levels of detail for specific audiences: an overview chart for senior management, a step schedule with task detail for the Core Team and leader, and task schedule with activity detail for individual Core Team members and the full project team working on these tasks.

Cycle-Time Guidelines

Cycle-time guidelines form the basis for project scheduling in world-class product development companies. Cycle-time guidelines are essentially the characterization of a company's product development process from a time perspective. Cycle-time guidelines are established at the step level and vary based on the characteristics of the product being developed. For instance, mechanical design cycle times for low, medium, and highly complex products can be captured over time and used as a basis for estimation on new projects.

Project schedules can then be estimated by breaking the project down to the step level of detail and categorizing the product and project in terms of such characteristics as complexity, technical risk, and scope. Step cycle times can then be estimated using these characteristics from a data base of cycle times. The overall project schedule is then completed using these step cycle times as building blocks.

Cycle-time guidelines provide an accurate method for developing reliable project schedules. Using them to develop step estimates, then using those estimates to generate accurate and predictable schedules, often boosts management's confidence in the team. Discussions between individual Core Teams and management focus on technical content and complexity instead of arguments over how much schedules are padded.

Cycle-time guidelines allow management to focus on the complexity of the product being developed. Discussions between management and Core Teams are no longer based on how much the schedule has been padded or how much management will arbitrarily cut out. Rather, everyone focuses on the complex characteristics of what has to be done.

Finally, cycle-time guidelines are a way to see if the process is being continually improved. World-class companies revise their cycle-time guidelines at least once a year because actual development times are being reduced continually.

Summary

The activities involved in developing products become more efficient and reliable when they are structured. The following points are important to recognize regarding product development structure:

- There are many clear symptoms that show the need for more structure.

- Balance between no structure and too much structure is essential.
- Within PACE, product development work is structured hierarchically into phases, steps, tasks, and activities.
- Three-level scheduling is an effective approach within this structure.
- Cycle-time guidelines are essential building blocks for scheduling.

6

Product Strategy
and New Product
Innovation

All companies would like to have a brilliant product strategy that enables them to enter an emerging market before anyone else or provides them with a continuous stream of competitively superior products. An effective product strategy can inspire the development of successful products; an ineffective product strategy makes even the best development efforts a waste of time. Brilliant or ineffective, product strategy is where product development usually starts, and it affects product development in many important ways.

Product strategy provides a strategic-level understanding of product opportunities. Without an effective understanding of product opportunities at a strategic level, a company is forced to make decisions on new products without seeing the entire spectrum of new opportunities. Without this visibility, mediocre products can be developed while better opportunities are overlooked.

With an effective product strategy, a company can be confident that it has considered all major opportunities before initiating its new product investments. Contrary to what may be thought, this consideration does not require extensive technical or market research; rather, it involves scanning the strategic horizon in order to inventory and classify opportunities.

Product strategy provides the link between a company's overall strategy and its product development. Through this link, strategic goals are translated into specific product objectives and development schedules in the Phase Review Process. Product strategy determines which opportunities enter Phase 0 of the Phase Review Process and influences which projects receive resource priority.

In the PACE process, product strategy is implemented through the Phase Review Process, but interestingly, it is frequently the Phase Review Process that drives the need for a better product strategy. This happens when senior managers or the Product Approval Committee (PAC) are faced with a formal Phase Review decision on a new product and realize that they don't clearly understand their company's product strategy. They struggle to establish priorities while feeling uncomfortable about having identified the best opportunities.

Product strategy provides a vision of where product development is going. Without a vision, there is no context for product developers. They end up defining products without a view of where each fits into future plans. The products they develop typically have too many or the wrong features, instead of being competitively positioned. Without the context that a vision provides, development takes place one product at a time, rather than as a coordinated strategy, and the result is a patchwork of individual products rather than an integrated product line.

This vision encourages proactive rather than reactive product development by systematically structuring future product development activities in advance, anticipating market and technical changes. Without such a vision, each new product proposal becomes a knee-jerk response to changes in the market. Additionally, this vision helps to identify the needs and priorities for technology development so that a company can effectively leverage its technological abilities.

Good product strategy creates more successful products, but what are these characteristics of product strategy that lead to more successful products? Our experience, as well as the many studies done on this issue, point to two primary characteristics of successful product strategies: leveraging a company's technical and marketing experience, and identifying products with a customer-based performance advantage. These characteristics were defined as two of the major determinants of product success in perhaps the best study on this topic. The study, which was conducted by M.A. Maidique and B.J. Zirger as part of an innovation project at Stanford University, looked at 158 products in the electronics industry—half successes and half failures.[1]

Most successful new products are based on a strategy of leveraging a company's technical or marketing skills. Without leverage a company does not have any inherent advantage. It is simply providing capital and human resources. With leverage a company brings specific advantages to either the development or marketing of the new product. This was the case with Intel in 1969. While developing custom calculator chips for a Japanese company, it invented the microprocessor. Realizing that it did not have the resources necessary to design the number of chips required for a wide variety of calculators, Intel tried to reduce the number of chips by implementing the more complicated steps as programs in memory rather than as hardware logic. The result was the first microprocessor—the Intel 4004—that equaled the computing power of the first electronic computer, the ENIAC, which filled 3000 cubic feet with 18,000 vacuum tubes.[2]

While a performance-to-cost advantage measures the extent of innovation in a new product and therefore indicates potential competitive advantage, if the superior performance is based on an in-depth understanding of customer needs, it yields real competitive advantage. This is the type of performance that the customer and the marketplace want and the type of product that is identified in a good product strategy.

Product strategy defines clear and consistent product positioning. Successful positioning of a product against competitive products usually comes from one of three product strategies: a product-price advantage, a superior product differentiation, or a product that is better focused on a segment of the market. In most cases, competitive positioning can be the difference between the success and failure of a new product.

Product strategy built around a product-price advantage has been typically associated with successful Japanese consumer-electronics companies that exploited product-cost advantages in their initial market penetration. A product differentiation strategy is exemplified by Cray, which originally differentiated itself by building the world's fastest computer. Market-segment focus has also led to many success stories. Bill Foster, the founder of Stratus Computer, credits his company's success on its "focus on its niche, the on-line transaction market."

Business strategy textbooks describe many approaches to strategy formulation involving new products, and product strategy can have many facets and dimensions, depending on the company and the industry. While these are all important in describing how to formulate product strategy, our focus here is more specific—how product strategy identifies the opportunities for new products and establishes both the boundaries and the priorities for making the decisions necessary to achieve product and cycle-time excellence.

New product opportunities can be identified in two different directions: through the expansion of existing product lines and through the innovation of new product lines. As part of the PACE process, we have developed product strategy frameworks to facilitate setting product strategy in each of these directions by scanning the horizon of opportunities in a structured manner. These frameworks enable a company to identify alternative opportunities and provide a common terminology for screening the alternatives.

Product strategy does not end with identifying and screening alternative opportunities. Products need to be designed to achieve a competitive advantage in the market, and this requires competitively positioning new products from the very beginning of development. Product positioning, integrated throughout the PACE process, begins with product strategy.

Product-Line Expansion

Opportunities for expanding current product lines are defined through product-line planning. When formally applied to each product line, product-line planning creates a time-phased series of conditional actions for developing new products and improving existing ones. Product-line planning includes strategically identifying opportunities for expanding the product line and mapping the product line both historically and as planned.

A product-line plan is *not* a detailed product specification. It should cover a three- to five-year time period, beginning the year in which products started today are expected to be completed. A product-line plan that defines products needed in the near future is not constructive unless those products are already under development. The time frame for product planning also underscores the benefit of having shorter cycle times for product development; companies with longer development cycles have much less flexibility and can only implement product strategy further in the future.

Identifying Opportunities for Product-Line Expansion

Many companies have found the framework presented in Figure 24 to be helpful in categorizing strategic opportunities for expanding a product line. It defines the possible new-product moves that can be made within the product line.

Five basic directions for product-line expansion are bounded by limits imposed by distribution constraints and competition. When the price gets too low, new distribution channels may need to be used, and at some point there may be no effective distribution channel. Higher-priced, lower-performance products are obviously noncompetitive. Each of these five basic directions has different objectives and requires a different approach.

1. *The low-end product targets a new market segment by offering a product that is more affordable to a new group of customers.* Typically, it provides reduced functionality at a lower price, which enables a company to either open up a new segment of the market or compete better in the low-price segment. To succeed with a low-end product, a company must design the proper mix of functionality and understand the potential in this market segment. Usually neither innovation nor advanced engineering is necessary.

Intel Corporation has demonstrated an example of a low-end product with the 386SX microprocessor, a stripped-down version of the company's 386 microprocessor. Internally both process 32 bits of data at a time, but the low-end 386SX can send and receive only 16 bits of data at a time instead of 32.

The differences between existing products and a new low-end product need to be real. If these are artificial performance restrictions, then competitors may be able to achieve an advantage by eliminating the artificial differences. Intel also provides a curious example of this with its 486 microprocessor and the related low-end version, the 486SX, introduced in the spring of 1991. The 486 has a built-in math coprocessor, while the 486SX is the same component at half the price with the math coprocessor disabled. Because Intel expected that it would be a year before competition could clone the 486/486SX, it could defer the threat of a competitor introducing a cheaper 486SX equivalent designed without the coprocessor. Interestingly, if a customer wants to upgrade to a 486

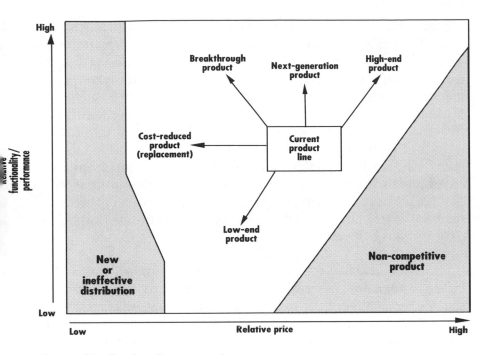

Figure 24. Product line expansion.

from a 486SX. Intel sells a 487SX, which is called a math coprocessor but is actually a regular 486 that disables the original 486SX when it is installed.

The low-end product-line extension must clearly have less functionality or reduced performance from current products or it will cannibalize sales of existing products. One company ran into this problem when it directed a project team to develop a new low-end version of its current products. The team defined a product that had all the primary features of the existing product but at a price 20% lower. When the team presented its concept for the product at the Phase 0 review, the PAC realized that it would significantly cannibalize existing sales and reduce rather than increase revenue.

2.   *Cost-reduced products are intended to replace current products in order to make them more price-competitive and extend their product life.* Typically, a cost-reduced product is developed by reengineering

the current product to take advantage of advances in technology such as integrated electronics and improvements in manufacturing. In some industries, such as personal computers, price erosion is so rapid that a combination of cost reduction and higher performance is needed to maintain sufficient profit margins.

In most cases a cost-reduced product is not even identified to customers as a different product; it simply has new internal designs and components. The cost of products can be reduced in many ways, including taking advantage of lower component costs, redesigning with less expensive materials, and redesigning them to be cheaper to manufacture. Some companies plan cost-reduced products at regular intervals during the product life cycle as part of a continuous cost reduction program.

3. *High-end products are typically designed with new features and higher-performance characteristics.* They appeal to the segment of the market that is willing to pay more for these advantages. High-end products do not immediately replace other products in the product line; they open new segments and interest existing customers to trade up to newer products. After a while, however, they may begin to replace previous products by becoming the new expected level of performance.

An example of a new high-end product was the IBM PC XT, which was introduced two years after the original PC and featured a hard disk plus other performance improvements. Another high-end product, the PC AT, was introduced a year after that with an improved microprocessor, more advanced diskette drive, and other features.

4. *Next-generation products replace the current product line with products that have higher performance and better functionality but at a similar relative price.* In almost all cases these products are based on new technology; otherwise they would be considered new high-end products instead of next-generation replacements. The distinction between high-end products and next-generation products is critical. Frequently companies do not themselves understand which type of product they are developing. The initial price of the next-generation product may be higher than the product it is replacing, since the price of the replacement product has eroded.

Usually a next-generation product provides a new platform for future products. This platform usually incorporates new technology that makes it superior to current products, and all future products will be based on this new platform.

The IBM PS/2, introduced in April 1987, was a next-generation product that replaced the IBM PC product line. The PS/2 was a much more sophisticated design than the PC AT. It was sleek and introduced VGA (video graphics array) video technology that gave improved resolution. It broke from previous PC/XT/AT standards by using the Micro Channel Architecture. Therefore, it could not use expansion cards developed for the previous products. Most importantly for IBM, this generation of PCs used more technology proprietary to IBM—roughly 80% in the PS/2 compared to 30% in the PC. IBM sold one million PS/2 personal computers within the first seven months.

5. *Breakthrough products are exceptional in that they both increase functionality and performance and reduce the relative price.* Breakthrough products almost always establish the starting point for new product lines because they tend to make existing products obsolete. True breakthrough products are rare, because most companies prefer to position a new product line as next-generation products with a premium margin. For this reason most breakthrough products are developed by new market entrants.

Personal computers represented breakthrough products in the word-processing market. They simultaneously provided additional functionality (they could perform tasks in addition to word processing), and they provided word processing at a lower cost. Companies such as Wang, which sold word processing systems, were hit hard by these breakthrough products.

The IBM System/360 product line introduced in 1965 was also a breakthrough product. It introduced the revolutionary feature (at that time) of upward compatibility and achieved dramatic new price performance. Compatibility enabled different sized computers to use the same software and connect to the same disk drives, printers, and other peripherals. The performance improvements came from advanced microcircuitry, which enabled 100,000 computations at the cost of about 3.5¢ compared to the previous cost of $1.38.[3]

Product-Line Mapping

Product-line mapping provides a time-phased view of the evolution of a product line. When applied historically, it explains reasons for the evolution, identifies strengths and weaknesses in the product-line strategy, and indicates the use of leverage. It is a way of evaluating the success of a company's product-line strategy and the implementation of that strategy.

When done prospectively, product-line mapping defines a time sequence of conditional moves to develop new products within a product line. It depicts the strategy for a product line by showing its planned evolution. The planned evolution provides a context for individual development efforts by showing how each planned product development is positioned relative to others and establishing relative priorities among potential development projects.

The Macintosh Product Line

The evolution of Apple's Macintosh product line presents an interesting illustration of how a product line evolves (see Figure 25). The Lisa was the forerunner of the Macintosh product line. The Lisa used the 32-bit Motorola 68000 microprocessor, user interface, and graphics capabilities that evolved into the Macintosh.

After the Lisa was introduced with a lot of fanfare in mid-1983, however, its weaknesses became apparent. Even though the Lisa used a 32-bit microprocessor, it was slower than the IBM PC because its extensive graphics capability consumed so much of the higher processing power. At $10,000 it proved to be too expensive. Additionally, it lacked sufficient software and couldn't be networked. As a result of these failings, Lisa sales dropped three months after introduction, leaving Apple with capacity that far exceeded demand.

The Macintosh was introduced in January of 1984 at a price of $2,495. The Macintosh used the Motorola 68000 microprocessor but also introduced the 3 1/2–inch disk drive. The drive was made for Apple by Sony, which had first introduced the drive two years earlier in its unsuccessful entry into the personal computer

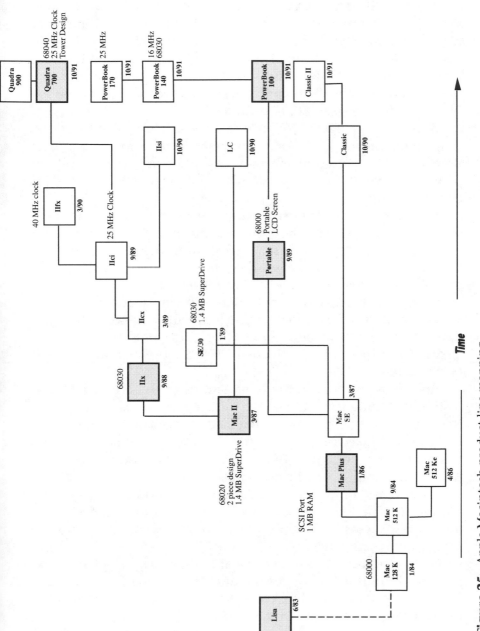

Figure 25. Apple Macintosh product line mapping.

market. (Sony sold only 1,600 computers in the United States before the product was withdrawn.)

The Macintosh was an immediate success. Apple sold 50,000 in the first 74 days. Initial problems due to its limited 128 K memory were overcome when the 512 K version was introduced in September 1984, four months earlier than expected. By the end of 1984, however, sales of the Macintosh began to slow. Apple was selling only approximately 20,000 units per month when it had been expecting to sell between 60,000 and 85,000.[4]

At the beginning of 1986, the Macintosh Plus was introduced. It included cursor keys and a numeric keypad for spreadsheet users as well as internal memory expandability to one million bytes. Fortunately for Apple, Microsoft had just released Excel for the Macintosh.

In March of 1987 Apple introduced the second Macintosh generation: the Macintosh II and the Macintosh SE. The Macintosh II was an open design for advanced applications with a built-in hard disk, color display, and network connections. Work had actually started on this product back in 1984. The Macintosh SE (system expansion) included additional internal memory and an internal slot for additional functions. It was specifically targeted at business users. Apple saw the development of these products as a race against the introduction of the new IBM PS/2 product line which it beat by a month.

Apple has introduced many variations of the original Macintosh II, including the IIx and IIfx, which were not successful. The IIfx was a high-priced product that sold fewer than 36,000 units in its first year.[5] Likewise, Apple's entry into the portable market was less than successful. The 14-pound MAC portable sold fewer than half of the number of units expected.

The low end of the market proved to be a good segment for the Macintosh. The Mac Classic, an entry-level product at $995, has been a big success, exceeding everyone's expectations. Interestingly, Apple considered a low-cost Macintosh back in 1984, but instead of expanding its product line at the low end, it opted for expanding into the higher-performance higher-margin segments. The Macintosh product line could have been much more successful with earlier expansion into the low end.

In October of 1991, Apple launched a number of new products, including a higher-performance Classic; the Classic II; its first notebook computer, the PowerBook™; and a new high-performance line, the Quadra. The PowerBook™ was designed for Apple primarily by engineers at Sony. They were able to complete this project in 13 months from a half-page specification.[6] The PowerBook™ 100 weighed five pounds, had two megabytes of memory, and was priced at $2,300. The PowerBook™ 140 and PowerBook™ 170 are more powerful versions of the same product.

It appears from this analysis that Apple has expanded and enriched its Macintosh product line much more in the past two years than it did previously.

New Product-Line Innovation

Expansion into totally new new product lines can be the most exciting type of product development. This is usually how rapid growth is achieved and is what is traditionally viewed as innovation. Identifying the best opportunities for new product lines is also the most difficult function of product strategy since the potential opportunities are vast and the risks are high.

As was stated earlier, a new product line is most successful when it leverages a company's existing strengths in marketing and technology. By leveraging its strengths, a company creates advantages to offset the challenges of a new product line. Conversely, history has shown a high failure rate for new product lines without this leverage. In spite of this, many companies attempt new product lines without much planning or forethought.

PRTM developed the framework in Figure 26 to help companies target opportunities for innovating new product lines. It positions new product-line opportunities on two dimensions: product technology and market/distribution channel. The product-technology dimension goes from the same product to similar products, to the same or similar technology, to completely new technology. The market dimension goes from the same market and distribution channel, to new markets through the same distribution channel, to completely new markets and distribution channels.

Current product line(s) are positioned in Figure 26 as the starting point in the lower left-hand corner. From there a company can move in three directions to introduce new product lines. The boundaries for success in these directions are usually limited by

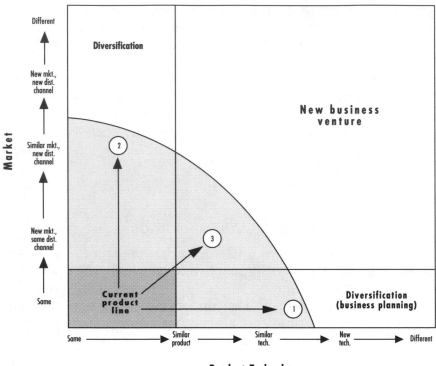

Figure 26. Framework for targeting new product lines.

the shaded area. Beyond these boundaries a company loses the benefit of leveraging its experience.

Texas Instruments (TI) illustrates some good examples of this framework. In 1975, as calculators were becoming commodity items, TI looked for new opportunities to apply the technology it had developed. TI initially targeted the increased use of calculators in the classroom environment and developed a product that included a calculator and math instruction book that was aimed at improving classroom learning. The company marketed this package directly to school systems—an example of a similar product sold to a completely new market through a new distribution channel, one that was outside TI's expertise. Within the framework shown in Figure 26, this effort went beyond the lightly shaded boundary and was a clear failure.

After this, however, TI pursued a more targeted approach and identified a similar product opportunity for a new market (children learning math) through its existing distribution channels (consumer electronics stores). The Little Professor was an electronic flash card, a calculator in reverse. It presented the problem and the child provided the answer. Introduced in August 1976 for less than $20, the Little Professor was tremendously successful. TI could not make enough of them for the 1976 Christmas season. TI expanded the Little Professor product line with products like Dataman in 1977.

TI subsequently targeted a new product line that leveraged the Little Professor by introducing a new product aimed at the same market but also introduced new technology—speech synthesis. The TI Speak and Spell, for example, a talking device that helped children learn how to spell, came out in mid-1978. It was also tremendously successful. TI has continued to build and expand this product line for more than 15 years.

Using the framework in Figure 26, a company can look for new product-line opportunities in three primary directions. Each of these leverages different strengths and offers different opportunities.

1. *Similar/new technologies and same market/distribution channel.* Targeting a new product line along these parameters has been a successful method of expansion for many companies. This form of innovation can be customer or technology driven.

Hewlett-Packard and Lotus together provide two examples of this type of new product-line innovation with the HP95LX, Jaguar product. It is an 11-ounce palmtop computer, priced at $699 that functions as a calculator and has Lotus 1-2-3 built in. It has the power and memory of many desktop PCs and a 16-line, 48-character screen. Jaguar's target market is the 14 million users of 1-2-3 and ten million customers of HP's calculator products who want the power of 1-2-3 in a portable package. Some analysts expect that it will double HP's calculator revenues.[7]

For HP it provides a new product line that can be sold to many of its existing customers through its existing distribution channels. It involves some new technology such as its infrared eye for transmitting data and plug-in cards, but it also leverages HP's 15 years of experience with the ergonomic, display, and electric power requirements of calculators.

For Lotus it provides 1-2-3 in a completely different package, one that encourages customers to have two copies of 1-2-3; one for their desk and one for their pocket. It is sold to the same market but through a different distribution channel. The Jaguar uses 1-2-3 version 2.2 software but introduces it in a way that required some technical challenges.

In the consumer products industry, the Swiss Corporation for Microelectronics and Watchmaking Industries (Swatch) realized that it had saturated the watch market and looked to related products for the same market. It leveraged its skills in designing products that are fun and easy to use and combined this with relatively simple telecommunications technology to develop the Swatch Twinphone. This unique product enables two people to use the phone at the same time. It targets the same type of customer who buys Swatch watches and is sold through the same distribution channels. New product-line innovation targeted at this same market includes a pager watch.

2. *Similar product and new market/distribution channel.* Expanding into new markets or distribution channels usually requires some product variation, but the emphasis is on new markets. Several examples illustrate this.

Microsoft introduced the Excel spreadsheet for the Macintosh in May 1985. By 1987 it captured 89% of the Macintosh spreadsheet market.[8] A version of Excel for the IBM PC market was an obvious new product opportunity, and development began shortly after the Macintosh version was released. In October 1987 the PC version of Excel was released. This provides an example of a similar product developed for an entirely different market.

Sun Microsystems announced plans to adapt its computer operating system to run on other computers. Scott McNealy, Sun's president believes that "Sun is sitting on a huge market opportunity." It is taking a similar product, its SunOS operating system, adapting it, and selling it into an entirely new market: other companies' microcomputers. When looked at as a separate market, Sun sold approximately 150,000 operating systems in 1990 compared to 5.2 million Microsoft MS-DOS and 333,000 IBM OS/2 systems. For Sun this is a new market that clearly requires a new channel of distribution since it is selling them to run on other computers.[9]

In another example, Sony is expanding into audiovisual systems for a new market—individual entertainment systems on board airplanes. Its ACCES in-flight entertainment system provides personalized film and music entertainment, video games, and flight information for each passenger.

3. *Combining similar/new technologies and related markets.* The most fertile area for innovation is based on a combination of similar and new product technology for new markets using the same distribution channel. This expansion strategy leverages both technology and market experience to create new innovative markets. We have already seen an example of this in the TI Little Professor. Another example is the successful expansion of companies into the VCR product line.

In the early 1970s Matsushita, JVC, and Sony began expanding into the consumer market for video cassette recorders. They did this by leveraging their success in television and audio products while perfecting the new video recording technology originally developed by Ampex, RCA, and Toshiba for the broadcast industry. Matsushita, JVC, and Sony targeted a new market (those who wanted to tape television programs), using the same distribution channel (consumer electronics stores), and a combination of similar (consumer electronics) and new (videotape recording) technology. By 1983 these three companies had almost 60% of a nearly 20 million unit market.

Interestingly, Ampex squandered its capabilities in magnetic video recording by trying to expand into computer peripherals and consumer audio—areas that lie in the much riskier new-business-venture region on the framework shown in Figure 26.

Some companies have grown quickly, methodically exploiting this fertile area of innovation. Microsoft provides an example. Microsoft BASIC gave it a leadership position in the microcomputer language market. By 1979 sales reached $2.5 million. In 1980 it began to think about expanding beyond computer languages. In November 1980 Microsoft contracted with IBM to develop the operating system, DOS, for the new IBM PC. It was available when the PC was announced in August 1981.

Microsoft continued to leverage its technical abilities into new markets, this time applications software. A spreadsheet application, Multiplan, was released in August of 1982 for the Apple II and shortly thereafter for the IBM. In November 1983 Microsoft released its second application software product: Microsoft Word.

After many delays, Microsoft expanded into a new area, interface manager products, with the release of Microsoft Windows in November 1985. Although it encountered problems early in its life, by 1989 more than two million copies of Windows had been sold.[10]

Microsoft was able to grow rapidly by leveraging its technological capabilities and distribution channel experience into one new market after another. It didn't stray from a strategy of exploiting this fertile strategic area, which creates innovation by leveraging existing strengths.

Many innovation-driven companies use this or a similar framework to identify new product-line opportunities by targeting the most fertile areas. With small teams of scientists, engineers, and marketing experts they can identify and evaluate specific opportunities. Typically, companies evaluate many specific opportunities before selecting the best one.

The framework helps identify specific new product line opportunities by framing specific questions. How can a similar product be applied to a new market? What new markets can be reached through current distribution channels? How can the technology in the existing product be applied to similar products?

At the same time, the framework keeps companies from making mistakes. One company that wanted to expand into new product lines initiated development in the totally unrelated areas of diversification and new business ventures (the unshaded regions in Figure 26). These efforts involved both new technology and new channels of distribution. The expansion efforts failed while the company's competitors expanded into new, but related, products in the same or related markets. After understanding this framework, the company changed direction and looked for new opportunities in related products within existing distribution channels.

Competitively Positioning New Products

Although most salespeople and many product designers believe that they need to develop products that are better in all aspects *and* cheaper than competitive products, in real markets this is usually impossible. Yet most successful products are positioned to achieve a competitive advantage relative to other products in the market. Competitive positioning is an important aspect of both product strategy and the early phases of product definition.

In competitive markets there are only three successful positioning strategies for new products: price leadership, differentiation, and focus.[11] These three generic strategies underlie most successful products.

Product Positioning Based on Price Leadership

Products that are price leaders attract customers by being the best product value in the market. The price-leadership strategy can usually be pursued successfully by only one competitor in a market. This product positioning strategy is best typified by Japanese consumer electronics manufacturers and automobile manufacturers during the 1970s and 1980s. They introduced much lower-priced products and were able to capture a significant market share.

To be successful with this strategy, a new product must exploit all sources of cost advantage. Typically, it is a standard product with few features, the ones in which customers are more interested. The product is usually sold in high volumes to take advantage of scale economies in manufacturing and distribution. A company pursuing this strategy successfully must be the lowest-cost producer in the market. Therefore, in designing such products, it is necessary to take advantage of all opportunities for trading off cost reductions for value.

PC-clone manufacturers have been successful with this strategy. They offer a comparable product at a much lower price. Dell Computer grew to more than $500 million in revenue by offering a PC clone at a lower price. To be the lowest-cost alternative, Dell optimized its total cost—including selling costs by selling directly to end customers. Now as Dell is being attacked by even lower cost Asian manufacturers, it is extending this strategy by trying to provide the lowest total cost to customers by improving the effectiveness of its customer service.

In the microprocessor market AMD competes on price relative to Intel. It sells its Intel-compatible AM386 at a lower price than the slightly slower Intel 80386. The price difference in October

1991 was $190 compared to $200. Another knockoff introduced by Chips & Technologies was introduced at $180.[12]

For this strategy to be successful, a product must have parity or proximity to other products on the basis of differentiation. In other words, the price difference is not offset in higher-priced alternatives by other advantages that have a high perceived value by potential customers.

Product Positioning Based on Differentiation

Many products have succeeded by differentiating themselves from other products based on attributes perceived as important by potential customers. This uniquely positions products in the market and enables them to command a premium price. Differentiation can be derived from many factors, including the product itself, its delivery system, or services related to it.

Product differentiation must increase customer-perceived value to be an advantage. This is done by either lowering the customer's total cost or improving performance. During the 1980s, for example, NCR ATMs obtained a significant product advantage through differentiation. The company was able to achieve much higher quality, reliability, and availability levels for its ATMs compared with those available from competitors. This significantly reduced customers' total cost in using NCR's products and led to a rapid increase in market share.

Differentiation can be achieved through unique product design and characteristics, such as those in the Sony 8-mm format compact camcorders. The differentiation in size, picture quality, and recording time (two hours compared with 30 minutes) relative to VHS-format compact camcorders gave Sony a major product advantage. Sony was able to capture more than 50% of new sales with this differentiation.

Another form of differentiation is through performance advantages, such as those offered by the latest microprocessor in differentiating the newest high-end PCs. Compaq's ability to be first to market with the latest microprocessor gave it significant, albeit temporary, differentiation.

The Canon AE-1 35-millimeter camera achieved competitive advantage through ease-of-use differentiation. Similarly, Apple Macintosh computers differentiated themselves based on their user interface and proficiency with graphics. In technical products conformance to existing standards can be a differentiator. Such was the case with products that had the ability to run Unix in the early days of the emerging Unix market.

All too frequently companies fail to execute product differentiation successfully. They do not understand the product factors that the customer values and differentiate products on uniqueness that is not highly valued by the customer. In new markets it is particularly difficult to assess in advance what attributes customers will actually value until companies gain experience in the market.

Sometimes companies introduce *too much* differentiation into the product and confuse customers. This often occurs because it is easier to specify all possible features than to decide which are really most important. Typical of too much differentiation is where marketing generates a wish list of requirements for the product to do everything. Contrary to this, successful differentiation comes in picking the right features. As will be discussed in Chapter 8, quality function deployment (QFD) is a useful technique to help pick the right features.

Differentiation is usually costly. This is one of the drawbacks to having too many features instead of the right features. The cost of differentiation also varies by company because companies have different advantages in technology, economies of scale, and the ability to share costs with other similar products. When significant differentiation can be cost-effectively achieved and the source of differentiation stems from a particular advantage, the success of the product can be sustained. Motorola was able to do this with the MICRO TAC, its hand-held cellular telephone. It was clearly differentiated by its small size, achieved using advanced semiconductor technology that Motorola produced in its large semiconductor division.

The success of product positioning based on differentiation depends on maintaining proximity to the price difference between products positioned by price. In other words, the differentiation has to be worth a higher price. IBM and Compaq have continually fought this battle of proximity with PC clones. When differentiation came from the certainty that only a true IBM PC or highly compatible Compaq would run all PC software, the value of differentiation was high, and proximity was achieved at a 50% to 100% higher price. But when the only differentiation was superior service and stability of the supplier, proximity represented only a

10% to 15% higher price. When you can get two PCs for the price of one, you can have a spare, and service becomes less of an issue.

By the middle of 1991, Compaq was suffering from this lack of differentiation, and sales plummeted. For many years it had sustained continued differentiation, first on size and compatibility and then on the introduction of advanced performance. When the value of the differentiation diminished, however, it was unable to compete with lower-cost PCs.

This illustrates one characteristic of many high-technology markets: they frequently mature to the point where differentiation is almost impossible to sustain. At that point, cost-based positioning is most successful. Remember that calculators were originally high-technology, high-priced products sold based on feature differentiation.

Product Positioning Based on Focus

It is also possible to position a product by focusing it on a particular market segment with unique requirements. A product focused at a particular segment of the market must be designed to have specific advantages to customers in that segment. There are two variations of a focused strategy: price-based focus and differentiation-based focus.

A price-based focused strategy exploits the differences in product cost for a particular segment. Typically this involves different product designs or configurations that are optimized for customers in that segment. A small-company PBX is an example of a price-based focused product. With a six- to ten-line capacity, fewer features, and no expandability, its cost is optimized for that particular segment of the market. It has a lower operating cost than multiple telephone handsets without a PBX and is cheaper than the low-end version of a larger PBX.

A differentiation-based focused product strategy exploits feature, functional, or performance differences in a particular market segment. Supercomputing is a unique market segment where the fastest computing power is the most desired feature. While IBM had always dominated the high end of the computer market, Control Data segmented the market in 1963 and developed a powerful computer, the CD 6600. It delivered three times the power of IBM's most powerful computer, the STRETCH, and IBM had nothing even close to this in its product plans.

IBM's CEO, Tom Watson, Jr., was furious when this happened. He issued an angry memo asking how Control Data could have beaten IBM with "only 34 people including the janitor."[13] Eventually he realized that "supercomputers had become so highly specialized that even if we came up with a design equal to theirs, it would never fit in with the rest of our product line, our style of selling, our volume and profit targets, and so on. Control Data outsold us more than fifteen to one, and in the end we canceled our supercomputer program after delivering only a limited number of machines." Here Watson has clearly defined how the differentiation-based focused strategy works.

Fault-tolerant computers is a another good example of specialized products successfully targeted at a specific market segment. Stratus computer exploited a differentiation-based focused strategy in offering redundancy in its computers. This design appealed to companies in the transaction-processing industry, with their need to have their computers up and running 100% of the time. Compared to other computers such as IBM's, Stratus's fault-tolerant machines offered significant advantages to those who were willing to pay more for this unique feature.

Products based on a focused strategy can be threatened if the value of the focus diminishes or if the market segment grows so large that it can be subsegmented. Changing technology can particularly affect these conditions, and the fault-tolerant market is seeing this type of impact. Increasing reliability of general-purpose computers is deflating the premium that users who do not need absolute up time are willing to pay. Some believe that what used to be a price premium of 100% will drop to 10–15%. At the same time, the fault-tolerant market is beginning to subsegment into Unix-based and proprietary systems.

Impact of Product Positioning

Figure 27 shows the relationship between the four positioning alternatives. Historically, unsuccessful products are unable to achieve any positioning advantages. The price-leadership products provide a better value. The differentiated products appeal to customers who value that differentiation, and the more focused products have advantages in particular market segments.

Yet we have found in many cases when we run workshops on product strategy, that senior executives are often unclear about

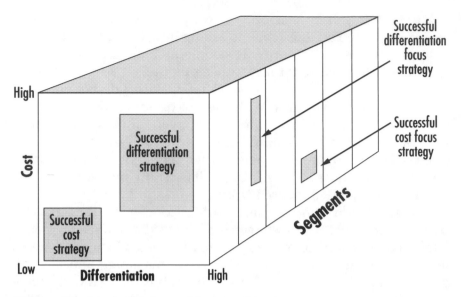

Figure 27. Successful competitive strategies.

how their company's products are positioned, nor, sometimes, can members of a product development Core Team agree on the positioning of the product they are designing. Product development teams need to have clear agreement early in the design phase on the positioning of the product they are developing.

A company's product strategy should define how it wants to position its products since it is difficult to maintain different positioning strategies within the same product line or even across product lines. For example, it is difficult for a company to maintain a price-leader product and highly differentiated product in the same product line.

Technology Change and Product Strategy

In most industries, technological change underlies new products. This change can open up new opportunities, make previously successful products obsolete, and turn upside down the competitive balance in an industry. As an example, Figure 28 plots the impact that changing technology has had on the cost of semiconductor memory prices.[14] Prices have declined by almost 95% in

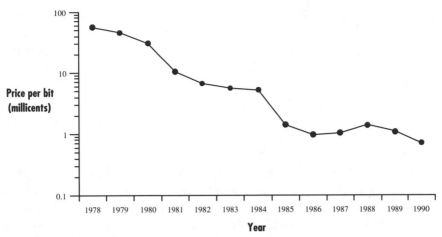

Figure 28. Dram price per bit comparison.

12 years. This technological trend has opened up a multitude of new product opportunities from PCs to video games.

There are three primary ways in which changing technology impacts product strategy.

1. *Changing technology creates opportunities and competitive pressure to change or expand products within a product line.* The faster the underlying technology in a product line changes, the faster that product line itself needs to change. In the personal computer and workstation markets, for example, advances in disk-drive, microprocessor, and memory technologies have significantly reshaped the market. Sun Microsystems, for example, has introduced eight generations of computers in the first nine and one-half years of its existence.[15]

To manage these opportunities and threats, companies must understand the trends in the key underlying technologies and potential new technologies that may reshape new products. For example, CD-ROM (compact disk read-only memory) technology may reshape products in the video game market. The technology provides a memory capacity 1,000 times greater than current game cartridges, and that will enable three-dimensional images, fluid animation, and superior sound. This technology has the potential to redefine the industry because Nintendo, the dominant player in the market because of its variety of game cartridges, is not strong in this technology. To compensate, Nintendo is pursuing a joint venture with Philips to develop a CD-ROM player.

2. *Changing technology provides opportunities to leverage technology into new products and markets.* As a company improves its capabilities in particular technologies and as those technologies become more advanced, opportunities for innovation in new product lines open up.

Motorola's MICRO TAC personal telephone was made possible by technological advances that the company had made in cellular technology and microelectronics.

Xerox developed new printer technology in its Docu-Tech publishing machines released in 1990, and it has begun to leverage this technology into other new product areas. The Xerox 4135, released in 1991, incorporates this new technology in a heavy-duty laser printer that prints 135 pages a minute, serving the market for mainframe-based printing such as credit card bills and insurance policies.

3. *Changing technology affects the success of product positioning.* Product positioning can be affected by changes in both product and process technology.

Products positioned for price leadership are most affected by technological changes that reduce component or material costs and by technological improvements in manufacturing that lower the labor or overhead required, reduce scrap, or improve quality. Companies with products positioned as price leaders usually need to be at the forefront of introducing these technologies. While they do not need to innovate these technologies, they cannot afford to get far behind in taking advantage of them.

Changes in microprocessor technology, for example, have created product advantages. Compaq Computer achieved a significant competitive advantage in late 1986 when it introduced a new computer based on the Intel 80386 processor—almost a year ahead of IBM's version of the 386 product. During that year Compaq sold tens of thousands of Deskpro 386 personal computers and clearly established itself as the leader in this high-performance segment with 80% market share. In 1987 Compaq's revenue doubled, from $625 million to $1.2 billion.

Cray Research, the leading maker of supercomputers, was unable to respond to technical change and felt competitive pressure when other companies introduced massively parallel computers based on a new technology that links hundreds of microprocessors together to perform calculations far more rapidly than Cray's conventional supercomputer. Cray was still three years away from developing a product with this technology after products from Thinking Machines and others had already been introduced.

Changes in technology that impact the basis for differentiation most significantly impact products positioned based on differentiation. New technology can make new features or functions possible, increase performance, or enhance reliability. The key here is to manage those technologies that impact the differentiating factors most important to customers.

Stardent Computer was a victim of this type of technological change. After investing $200 million, Stardent had developed a desktop computer with dazzling graphics and heavy-duty power. Changes in computer-chip technologies made it possible for popular workstations to do the same job at a lower cost. In October 1991, Stardent went out of business.

The rapid rate of technological change makes time to market even more important. In the electronics industry, for example, the best product designs based on old technology are generally not as competitive as an inferior design based on new technology, and the rate of technological change is rapid. Jack Kuehler, President of IBM, believes that semiconductor and other computer technologies will increasingly accelerate through the end of the century and that "if you don't keep up, you'll never catch-up."

Summary

Within PACE the focus of product strategy is on identifying the opportunities for new products and establishing both the boundaries and the priorities for making the decisions necessary to achieve product and cycle-time excellence:

- Product strategy has two different objectives: to plan the expansion of existing product lines and to identify opportunities for innovating new product lines.
- The framework presented in Figure 24 can be useful in categorizing strategic opportunities for expanding an existing product line.
- The framework presented in Figure 26 can be useful in targeting opportunities for new product lines.

- In competitive markets there are three primary strategies for positioning new products: price leadership, differentiation, and focus.
- Changing technology impacts product strategy by creating new opportunities and competitive pressure, providing leverage into new products, and affecting the success of product positioning.

References

1. Robert A. Burgleman and Modesto A. Maidique, *Strategic Management of Technology and Innovation* (Irwin, Homewood, Ill., 1988), p. 321.
2. Mariann Jelinek and Claudia Bird Schoonhoven, *The Innovation Marathon* (Basil Blackwell, Oxford, England, 1990).
3. Michael L. Tushman and William L. Moore, Editors, *Readings in the Management of Innovation* (Harper & Row, New York, 1988), p. 46.
4. John Sculley, *Odyssey* (Harper & Row, New York, 1987), p. 230.
5. Abby Christopher, "Herefore Art Thou, Apple?," *Upside,* October 1991, p. 38.
6. Brenton R. Schlender, "Apple's Japanese Ally," *Fortune,* November 4, 1991, p. 151.
7. Alan Farnham, "The PC You Put in Your Pocket," *Fortune,* May 20, 1991, p. 114.
8. Daniel Ichbiah and Susan L. Knepper, *The Making of Microsoft* (Prima Publishing, Rocklin, Calif., 1991) p. 169.
9. "Why Sun Can't Afford to Shine Alone," *Business Week,* September 9, 1991, p. 87.
10. Daniel Ichbiah and Susan L. Knepper, *The Making of Microsoft* (Prima Publishing, Rocklin, Calif, 1991) p. 169.
11. This framework was introduced by Michael E. Porter in *Competitive Advantage,* (The Free Press, New York, 1985).
12. Julie Pitta, "Live by the Clone, Die by the Clone," *Forbes,* October 28, 1991, p. 109–110.
13. Thomas J. Watson, Jr., *Father Son & Co.* (Bantam Books, New York, 1990).
14. Data from *Electronic Purchasing,* June 1991, and Integrated Circuit Engineering Corp.
15. *The Wall Street Journal*, September 5, 1991.

7

Technology Management

Imagine if every time you developed a product, the technologies you needed to meet its goals were sitting on a shelf, like modular building blocks, needing only to be selected and integrated with each other. Imagine that these were the best technologies, state-of-the-art, fully tested and debugged. Moreover, they were proprietary, well protected by patents, trade secrecy, and applications know-how only you fully possess. In short, imagine that technical uncertainty had been reduced to a bare minimum, to issues of how well you exploit your technology position, not whether it will do what is advertised or whether competitors can leapfrog you. What would be the impact of this dream condition on your development success rate and cycle time?

A major element of risk would have been eliminated from developing product strategy. You could select the right combinations of product performance, features, and cost to maximize your market share and return. Product line planning would be a matter of spacing out your winners and managing the pace of advance (avoiding, perhaps, getting too far ahead of your customer). Cycle times could be close to their theoretical minimum with the key issue being time-efficient execution. Product introductions would be highly predictable and the allocation of development resources would be easily optimized.

This is, of course, a pleasant fantasy, not a state that can be achieved fully. Technology uncertainty and risk are inescapable. They can't be made to disappear; they can only be managed. The point of this daydream is that even achieving a modest efficiency in the technology/product development interface can yield enormous reductions in development time and improvement in product success.

Technology Development and Time to Market

Effective technology development has enormous impact on time to market. Often when development times are long, a root cause is incomplete technology development or the need for extensive invention concurrently with development.

At a company making systems for processing high-resolution films we compared the cycle times of projects with differing levels of inventive content. All were complex multiyear developments based on highly proprietary technologies. In all the cases, new products were being developed, not minor enhancements of existing ones. What differed was the readiness of the underlying technologies. In some projects, the technologies were known; only the applications were new. We called these "low inventive content." In others, the underlying technologies were still under development and much invention was required. We called these "high inventive content."

Figure 29 shows the average differences in cycle time for more than a dozen projects, all with roughly equivalent projected schedules and budgets. The high inventive content projects took three times as long to complete overall as the low inventive content! There were two major differences. Once the product concept had been decided upon and significant resources devoted to the projects, the high inventive content projects took twice as long to complete. This is shown by the "time from concept to stable manufacturing" bar. Technical difficulties along the way led to many changes in direction and repetition of steps. The unpredictability of the invention portion of the work led to difficulties in keeping activities in their proper sequence. Some manufacturing process development activities preceded stabilization of the design, for example, and had to be redone after the products were initially introduced.

The second major difference in cycle time was at the beginning of the projects. The high inventive content projects took a long time to truly get going. It took as long from when the need for the products was identified to when the projects actually began as it took for the entire low inventive content development! Why did this happen? Because the degree of invention

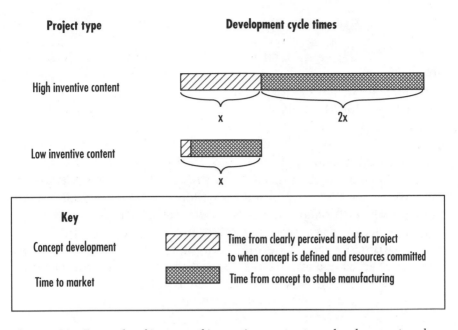

Figure 29. Example of impact of inventive content on development cycle time.

needed made it harder to clearly define product concepts that developers felt confident they could realize. Also, the risk associated with these projects made it harder to get management consensus quickly. Low levels of exploratory activity would begin while the organization waited for a champion to emerge, or the need became so pressing that pushing forward could be delayed no longer.

In addition to reducing time to market, technology strength affects product and business success. GTE has tracked core technologies and the competitive position of these technologies since the 1980s. The winning businesses have had strong technology positions relative to competitors. Those with weak core technology positions have rarely corrected themselves. At GTE and elsewhere, in our experience, effective management of technology is one of the key predictors of product and business success.

Are Ivory Towers the Answer?

Managing technology development is different from managing product development because technologists or research scientists are different from developers.

Recognizing this, many companies set their research activities apart, in separate R&D or central research organizations, so-called ivory towers. Some of these organizations—such as Bell Labs and the old RCA's Sarnoff Labs—have been highly productive. It could be argued that institutions such as these technologically spawned the Japanese electronics industry, which licensed invaluable technologies from these and other fundamental technology centers.

Many companies have extended the ivory tower principle to product development. One minicomputer company in a city with low commercial real estate rates decided to send a development team to a posh office complex apart from the regular engineering organization. For months this team met to define its next product far from the day-to-day pressures of the rest of the organization, but more importantly, far from the customer. The product concept changed many times. Should they develop a high-end feature-laden product or a low-cost one? Which technologies should be included in the design? Since the team had mostly technical people, it focused almost exclusively on technical issues, not marketing trade-offs. Months passed inconclusively. When management announced that the team members would move back to their old offices, suddenly they reached a compromise. The team would design a product that might appeal to both high-end and low-end users. When it was finally unveiled, of course, it appealed to neither. It was too expensive for the low end and not fast and powerful enough for the high end.

Setting developers apart in this way is rarely a good idea, although it often is productive for research scientists. Send scientists to the ivory tower and they may bring back superconductivity. Send developers to the ivory tower and they will bring back white elephants.

Researchers and developers are different, but they need each other. The best product developers in the world will fail without access to appropriate technology, and the best technologist will produce little of practical value without developers to use the technology in products addressing actual customer needs.

The Differences Between Researchers and Developers

To effectively manage both researchers and developers, it helps to recognize how their perspectives and activities differ.

1. *Time horizon.* The developer's natural focus is on *this* development, *this* project, a specifically targeted customer or market. The horizon of the researcher is much vaguer. The diffusion of technology is slow. Basic work done today might find its way into products years from now. Technologies ready for efficient deployment were developed years ago or are based on know-how developed years ago. In fact, almost nothing companies invest in has such a long-term impact. Technology development is the ultimate long lead time item. Technology development is investment in the future; product development is cashing in on past technology work. Technology development is an implicit statement about the long-term intentions of a company. (This is why patents are such a good source of competitive intelligence.) In this sense technology development is the most strategic of investments. Decisions made today about technology may define what you may develop long in the future.

2. *Basic orientation.* Good developers have customers in mind. They focus on what is technically possible to make the product meet a clear-cut set of needs of an identified set of customers. They watch environmental and regulatory trends and the evolution of standards. They may follow developments in technology, too, but largely to understand what will be possible soon, so they may exploit that possibility to satisfy a customer need.

Good researchers focus on creating new possibilities: better, faster, cheaper, or—in the extreme case of breakthroughs—something entirely new. They watch advances in fundamental science (or contribute to them) with an eye to discovering a practical application. New materials, new measurement capabilities, new algorithms, or new computing power means new classes of possibility.

Effective management of the technology/product development interface requires an understanding of the fundamental timing mismatch. Technology and development must be connected like a slow-turning, large gear to a fast-spinning small one with the right mechanism: a technology strategy.

3. *Key resource.* The key resource of researchers—what they really manage—is the skill base. It takes time to assemble experienced and productive technologists. Their areas of specialization are often the hot ones, so they can be difficult to hire. It takes time to develop their in-depth knowledge of a field and to gain practical experience. They may require specialized equipment, another investment.

It follows that a change in technology strategy likely implies or necessitates a change in the technical staffing mix. Some of this may be accomplished through retraining and redirecting people, but this is rarely enough. One of the greatest technology shifts of our time—that from largely electromechanical solutions to electronic ones—made obsolete whole R&D organizations. Companies that didn't make the shift were often weighed down by the sunk investment in mature technology. The task of technologically retooling was seen as too great or was delayed far too long.

For the developer the key resource is often the experience embodied in the structured development process. By streamlining the repeatable elements of the process and encouraging effective integration of the functions, execution is swift and efficient.

4. *Repeatability and predictability.* Researchers search for the novel, the unique, the serendipitous. Discovery is unpredictable and only barely repeatable. Discovery is not a random walk, however. If it were it would be so rare as to be miraculous. When a team invents a new class of pharmaceutical by altering a molecule, it is faced with a virtually infinite set of permutations. If the search were truly random, success would take nearly forever. Similarly, if luck or brute force solutions were the only bases of invention, scientists would almost never come up with multiple breakthroughs. Sir James Black, for example, discovered both the beta blockers and the H_2 antagonists. Some deep rules must apply, and in this case they were the notions of blocking specialized receptors and the conscious engineering of compounds. Such deep or overriding ideas are the key to productive research.

For developers, predictability is much higher. Good development processes increase the predictability of results, and companies can exploit that confidence strategically.

5. *Application.* Another fundamental difference lies in how work is applied. Technologies have broad applications, spanning many products and even industries. Development focuses on the specific application of technology to a specific product.

This difference profoundly affects how one must search for relevant technology and value it. Because technologies are broad in applicability (the broader, generally, the better) and even migrate from industry to industry, it is necessary to scan broadly to discover the relevant trends. A semiconductor substrate company, for example, solved a sticky problem in its molding operations by adopting a mature technology used in making popsicles.

The goal is *access* to appropriate technology, not necessarily internal development. Every technology decision is a make or buy decision. The internal bias toward make is strong, but it should be recognized that access to mature technologies from external sources is often the better choice. The cost or time required for internal development may be prohibitive. Even embryonic technologies can be acquired. Japan's reliance on licensed technology in its remarkable period of growth since World War II shows that an external technology wedded to world-class product development and manufacturing is a highly rewarding strategy.

A parallel risk is too much reliance on others for core technologies. We call this "as-if-invented-here." Many core electronics technologies are in the hands of suppliers, especially semiconductor firms. Some of the volatility of the market shares of electronics systems companies relate to their dependence on suppliers for the fundamental technologies that define product performance and cost. Who selects the right microprocessor or has access to low-cost memory may determine whose next generation machine makes it to market early.

In many industries, especially electronics and advanced materials, the balance between who pays for technology development and who captures the value added downstream often determines success and profitability.

6. *Financial value.* Estimating the financial value of technical activities for product development is easy. The return can in many cases be tied to the financial attractiveness of the specific application. Standard financial metrics, such as return on investment (ROI) or net present value (NPV) can be used to measure attractiveness.

Valuing core technologies is much more difficult. Much of what is being valued hinges on future applications of the technology. Standard metrics such as ROI or NPV are very hard to apply. Researchers tend to be overly conservative in projecting the timing and magnitude of financial return. Such numbers are difficult to defend.

The contingent nature of technology development makes predicting return especially difficult. Not every technology will be commercialized. While the expected value of such work can be calculated, it is hard to make it realistic.

Basic technology development often triggers unforeseen applications. The scientist who starts it all may have no more insight into the full sweep of opportunity than anyone else. In practice, if capital budgeting metrics are applied, they tend not to justify any basic technology development (except, notably, in pharmaceuticals, where a temporary patent and regulatory monopoly produce extraordinary returns, and perhaps in one or two other industries). Yet the result is counterintuitive. Does it really mean that it is not worthwhile to invest in technology development? No, it doesn't. What it does suggest is that the nature of technology development is different enough to justify a different kind of financial analysis.

Two approaches to valuing technology are available. One is quantitative, the other qualitative. The quantitative approach is based on an insight of Graham Mitchell, the Director for Planning for GTE Laboratories and Bill Hamilton, who teaches technology management at the Wharton School.[1] As Dr. Mitchell likes to put it, they realized that researchers were looking at the wrong page of the finance text. Instead of treating fundamental R&D as a straightforward investment on the capital budgeting model, they recommend treating it as a stock option. A stock option involves betting a small amount of money (the exercise price, which is a fraction of the purchase price) on the volatility of a stock. It may be exercised for a specified period of time. If the price goes up in time above the exercise price, the buyer of a stock option makes money. If it doesn't, all the buyer loses is the up-front money. The essence of a stock option is that the downside is fixed and the upside is unbounded.

This sounds a lot like investing in technology. The exercise price is the R&D investment, which is a small fraction of the total investment commercialization would require. The bet is that the technology will prove rewarding. The downside is fixed and the upside unbounded.

An investment in a specific product development or a manufacturing facility is more valuable the sooner it generates returns and, since most managers don't like risk, the more certain those returns. An option or technology bet is more valuable the *longer* it is possible to exercise it and *the more uncertain* (in the sense of volatility) the outcome. A technology investment that may address a vast commercial possibility (that is, big upside) for a long time to come is more valuable than one addressing a lesser possibility sooner. The reverse is the case, in general, for development or capital budgeting decisions.

A qualitative approach to managing technology is technology planning, a rational way of assessing where a company should place its technology bets.

Technology Planning: The Art of the Unbundling

The objective of technology planning is to address four questions in a concise and meaningful way:

1. Which technologies are relevant to the product line?
2. What is the character and potential of these technologies?
3. How do the technologies compare to those of competitors?
4. How can practical access to the needed technologies be gained?

To answer these questions so that they guide how technology resources are allocated requires a minimum of three assessments (shown in Figure 30):

- market criticality
- technology maturity
- technology competitive position

Many other useful concerns may be added, such as protectability of the technology (that is, can it be patented defensibly?) and the current level of investment in the technology. These deepen the understanding, but answering the three questions in Figure 30 are sufficient for decision making.

The technique of technology unbundling is an efficient way to

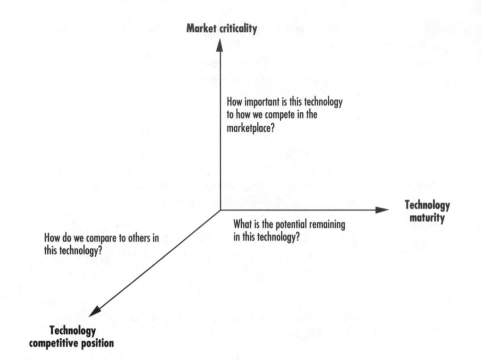

Figure 30. Assessing a technology: the minimum set of information required.

answer these questions. The technique is based on the insight that technologies are best identified in relation to products. Good product planning and technology planning go hand in hand. Companies such as 3M with its well-constructed technology roadmap process formally combine the two. QFD is another way to relate technical, market, and competitive considerations. It works well with technology unbundling.

Steps of Unbundling

Technology unbundling can be best understood as a series of five steps:

1. *Define the products.* A good way to begin is to identify representative products—current ones and/or ones under development

or consideration. These need to be defined fairly clearly in terms of features and positioning. The intended customer and the basis competitive positioning should be known. This helps to recognize which technologies are most important.

2. *Unbundle technologies.* Once the appropriate product definitions are identified, the relevant technologies can be *unbundled*. A typical unbundling will identify 20-30 technologies. They should include product and process technologies as well as vendor-supplied key components and assemblies. They should not be limited to those currently being used. Competing approaches, including those from outside the industry, should be included. The entire value chain should be reviewed for relevant technologies: in design and development, test, manufacturing, distribution, and service.

The output of this step is a list of the technologies that might be useful in designing the products defined. For complex systems this analysis may proceed at several levels: the system and major subsystems within it. Typically, only classes of critical components are identified.

3. *Assess market criticality.* Market criticality is the key competitive dimension. The criticality of the technology helps to answer some important questions. Does this technology help position products to better meet customers' needs? If a company competes on the basis of differentiation, does the technology improve its performance or enable it to offer new features or functionality? If it competes on the basis of low cost, does the technology fundamentally improve its economics?

Some technologies offer little opportunity to improve competitive positioning, but if misapplied or absent can hurt it. These are the *basic* technologies. Companies need them to be competitive, but superiority in them won't provide an advantage. Most technologies are basic and the best tactic is to address weaknesses in them but not to spend scarce resources to lead the field.

Other technologies are consistently critical to competitive positioning in the marketplace. These are the *core* technologies, the true market differentiators. Market leaders usually lead in these. Being better than competitors in core technologies usually translates into market advantage.

Finally, some technologies have the potential to alter the

game. These are the core technologies of the future. If they fulfill their potential (and uncertainty about that likelihood is often high), they become the competitive driver. These are the *future core* technologies, and access to them is often a matter of survival.

Table III summarizes the three classifications of market criticality: basic, core, and future core.

Technologies evolve in regular ways. Future or potential core technologies prove their usefulness or do not. If they do they eventually become core. Core technologies in various permutations may remain core for a long time. In time, however, as patents run out or as competitors learn to achieve the same results, they become basic. Sensitivity to this evolution keeps companies from overinvesting in basic (once core technologies) or underinvesting in future core technologies.

4. *Understand the maturity of the technologies.*[2] The literature of technology diffusion is full of s-curves. These trace the patterns of activity in a technology: a low embryonic stage, busy growth, an active but slowing mature stage, and finally aging. Maturity is a function of four things:

- potential
- level of activity
- uncertainty
- accessibility

As a technology matures its potential diminishes. By the aging stage it is quite small. Activity in a technology increases with each stage, then declines in the final stage. Uncertainty is highest at the outset when it is difficult to predict results and timing, then diminishes over time, rising perhaps slightly at the end as practitioners become scarce.

Accessibility—the ability to get the technology—is lowest in the embryonic stage, climbs in the growth stage, and is greatest in the mature stage, declining in aging. In the early stages internal development is of the most cost-effective approach. In the mature stage acquisition or other buy options such as licensing and contract development become attractive. What maturity reveals about make vs. buy is useful in helping this analysis reveal opportunities to more cheaply access needed technology.

Table III.   Market criticality: overview of basic vs. core technologies

Type	Ability to Provide Advantage	Current Degree of Application	Competitive Aim
Basic	Low	High	Maintain parity
Core	High	High	Lead and exploit
Future core	Potentially high	Low	Lead or guarantee access

5. *Assess technology competitive position.* This is a comparison of a company's strength with its technology competitors for the product technologies identified in the unbundling. Technology competitors include direct competitors but also may include customers, suppliers, or other technology centers of excellence. This breadth is valuable because a technology competitor may be a business ally. Technology-based alliances such as the relationship between IBM and Intel can be highly productive.

This comparison is difficult in general terms, but easier for a specific technology. There are many sources of comparative information. Based on experience and an understanding of the products of competitors, judgments are generally quite accurate. A simple scale of + meaning better than competitors, 0 meaning equal, and – meaning worse than competitors is used in Table IV, which shows a standard format for an unbundling.

Analyzing the Unbundling

An unbundling contains enormous information. Look at the overall pattern. Are there many future core technologies?

Table IV.   The technology unbundling format

Product Definition			
Technologies	Market Criticality	Technology Maturity	Technology Competitive Position
Technology$_1$	Base	Embryonic	+
Technology$_2$	Core	Growth	0
•	Future core	Mature	-
•	•	Aging	•
•	•	•	•
•	•	•	•
•	•	•	•
•	•	•	•
•	•		•
Technology$_n$			

Are current core technologies getting mature and hence played out? These are clues to likely technology-driven shifts.

Analyze the overall position and ask some key questions. Are you strong in all or most core technologies? Are you at least equal in most or all basic technologies? Are you investing in the most promising future core technologies?

In general, look at market criticality first, paired with technology competitive position. When there are weaknesses in basic or core technologies, look at maturity as a guide to whether internal development versus external access is best. Where there are conspicuous strengths in the core technologies, look to see if they are exploited well.

For future or potential core technologies, competitive position may be less telling. Look at maturity as an indicator of how soon the technology is likely to demonstrate its value. Then solve for competitive position, which is highly sensitive to the level of investment. The questions to ask about a future core technology include: How soon will it be available? How likely is it to deliver on its promise? How much investment will it take to develop? Will there be access if others develop it?

A manufacturer of cordless telephones identified the design of powerful lightweight batteries as a future core technology. The investment required to make a fundamental improvement was very high and difficult to justify for this application alone. Since the company did not intend to enter the battery business, it decided to establish relationships with the leading developers of advanced batteries to guarantee early access to new battery technology.

Technology Strategy

An analysis of the type described can help translate market and technology insight into a practical technology strategy. It will help determine viability as a competitor and which technologies must be added or reinforced. Most of all it can help assure that the technologies required to develop products are available when needed. This can have enormous impact on cycle time.

Example of Technology Unbundling

A consumer electronics company was diversifying into marine electronics, a field that would exploit many technical skills it already possessed but require many new ones. Some preliminary development work had begun, but there was uncertainty about how well positioned technically this firm was to develop successful new products. It decided to unbundle the new marine product. About 30 technologies were identified. Some of the required technologies were those the company knew very well. These included signal processing software development and design for miniaturization. Others were virtually unknown. The new product would be partly submerged, and the firm knew little about how to retard marine growth, a big problem for marine products. Other parts of its products would be exposed to salt air and water and it knew little about corrosion resistance or waterproofing. Advanced sonar technology would be needed based on techniques used by the Navy.

Overall, about 12 core technologies were identified. The company was weak in six of these. This led it to question its ability to succeed.

Rather than cancel the project, executives elected to put product development on hold while they addressed the core technologies. They began a research program and after a modest investment, concluded that the effort required to master these new technologies was too great. A costly and probably lengthy development was averted. The company funneled resources into core technologies supporting its other businesses. This led to several new products.

PACE and Technology Management

Much of this chapter has been focused on the way technology management differs from product development. PACE helps companies to manage these differences in two important ways.

First, PACE establishes clear definitions of projects, the PACE boundaries. By clearly separating technology from product development projects there is little chance that the former will be forced into an inappropriate structured development process.

Secondly, at every phase review, the issue of technical risk or the degree of invention is reviewed. When it is clear that the risk is very high, the PAC considers risk reduction options. If the product development project can be delayed, a technology development program may be substituted. Only when it succeeds are products developed. If product development cannot be delayed, other ways of reducing technical risk are considered. For example, the missing technology may be licensed or a simpler version of the product may be developed immediately *without* the new technology while the technology is developed concurrently for use in second generation products.

When PACE techniques such as these are used, the technology/development interface is enormously improved. One developer compares a good technology/development interface to a smoothly running train schedule. Each product development project is a train about to leave the station. It has a tight schedule but may load anything ready to go at the time of departure and meet its scheduled time of arrival. Any technologies ready for application can board this train. Any still being developed must wait for the next. Because the schedule is tight and the railroad efficient, the next train is already in the schedule, the product line plan. Missing a train is no tragedy; another will be coming along soon. The net effect is short cycle time and effective technology development. Developers don't slow down to wait for unfinished technology, and the technologists work to get their contributions ready for clearly anticipated applications. After all, they don't want to miss too many commercialization vehicles.

We've often observed the vicious cycle of slow development times leading to pressure to catch up in the next product. Such pressure increases technical risk enormously and usually leads to protracted developments and further pressure to catch up.

Discipline in avoiding (except as an extreme resort) regular reliance on invention can produce the opposite effect, a virtuous cycle. Short cycle times encourage more modest incorporation of new technology, which encourages continuing short cycle times and a flowing pipeline of technology advances, including inventions.

Companies rely on a mix of major advances and incremental ones. Too much reliance on major advances leads to an unacceptable rate of product failure; too much reliance on incrementalism may lead to sterility and vulnerability to obsolescence. A development process that recognizes the different resource requirements and timing of major new high-risk programs and incremental lower risk programs can accommodate both in the same organization.

Maintaining a clear distinction between technology and product development, despite the ease with which they masquerade as each other, will improve both.

Summary

Technology management sets the stage for many of the other elements of product development. The following highlight its role and importance:

- Effective technology management can greatly reduce development cycle time and improve product success rate.
- Technology management must be based on clear understanding of the differences between technology and product development.

- Technology planning based on such techniques as unbundling should guide the allocation of resources.
- A disciplined technology/development interface will encourage pull for appropriate technologies and rapid time to
  market.

References

1. For more detailed treatment of these ideas, see Graham R. Mitchell
   and William F. Hamilton, "Managing R&D as a Strategic Option," *Research Technology Management*, Vol. 31, No. 3 (May-June 1988).
2. For more detailed discussion of the concept of technology maturity,
   see Philip A. Roussel, "Technological Maturity Proves a Valid and Important Concept," *Research Management*, Vol. 27, No. 1 (January—
   February 1984).   These ideas and the technology classification
   schemes pioneered by John Ketteringham and others at Arthur D. Little, Inc., have informed our work in this chapter. See also *Third Generation R&D*, Philip Roussei, Kamal Sabd, Tamara Erickson, Harvard
   Business School Press, 1991.

8 ▦▶

Design Techniques and Automated Development Tools

Historically, improvements to the product development process have focused on the application of various design techniques and automated development tools. Often touted as silver bullets, these tools and techniques promised dramatic improvements in time to market, product quality, and engineering productivity. Unfortunately, many companies investing in a specific tool or technique found that improvements were minimal. Often the disappointing results were attributed to flaws in the tool or technique, when in reality fault was due to improper application.

PACE looks at product development as a process with many aspects that should be improved, not as something that can be fixed by the application of a lone tool or technique. Techniques such as quality function deployment (QFD) and the various techniques encompassed by design for excellence (DFE) can dramatically impact product development but only when applied correctly within the structured process. Automated design tools can be used to support core team effectiveness through improvements in design in specific functional areas and through integration of the technical aspects of product development.

After a company has implemented the basic elements of PACE (Core Teams, Phase Review Process, and a Structured Process Development), the appropriate application of specific tools and techniques can lead to tremendous reduction in time to market and lower life-cycle costs. Applying these tools and techniques before the basic elements of PACE are functioning will only lead to disappointment.

Design Techniques

In recent years several major design techniques have been developed with the objective of improving the effectiveness and productivity of design professionals. The major techniques include quality function deployment (QFD), the array of techniques encompassed by design for excellence (design for assembly, manufacturability, testability, serviceability, international, and green) and user-oriented design. Each technique, when properly applied within the context of PACE, can lead to additional improvements in the product development process.

Simplified Quality Function Deployment (S-QFD)

Quality function deployment (QFD) is a technique originally developed by the Kobe Shipyard in Japan during the 1970s. It is a disciplined approach to planning, communicating, and documenting customer requirements and translating them into design activities. Many excellent books and articles on QFD explain the concept;[1,2] here we will focus on a more simplified approach to QFD.

Traditional QFD focused on elements of a relatively simple product. Capturing customer requirements and design alternatives was straightforward and did not take much time. When attempting to apply the technique to complex system products, however, PRTM found classical QFD to be quite cumbersome and time consuming. We spent almost two years modifying the basic QFD approach to work more effectively with more complex products.

When there are many elements to consider, such as in a systems product containing many hardware and software subsystems, different customer requirements, a high degree of complexity, and short life cycles, QFD tends to lengthen time to market. The value of QFD quickly diminished after identifying high-level requirements and prioritizing them. If the problem is complex, it is easy to get lost in the process of a QFD analysis. For example, design teams at one company found that their lists of customer requirements and technical approaches often resulted in matrices that had hundreds of columns and rows, leading to thousands of cells to evaluate. Clearly a new and different approach was required. PRTM developed simplified quality function deployment, or S-QFD, in 1989 and has since refined and applied the technique on many complex technology-based products.

S-QFD begins with what is termed *voice of the marketplace* (VOM). We use the term *marketplace* instead of *customer* because most technology-based companies have many "customers" that they must satisfy, such as the sales force, system integrators, end-users, regulatory agencies, and international standards. Essentially, voice of the marketplace means describing what each of these customers wants in their own language. Voice of the marketplace information includes cost, performance, ease of use, features, appearance, size, and compliance with standards among a host of other elements. This information has to be gathered first internally, from those in close contact with customers such as sales, customer service, and marketing; and then externally by talking to present and potential customers.

Properly employing S-QFD can increase the enthusiasm of the design team. "Even engineers like to know that they are building products that people want to buy," notes Bob Hinden, a Core Team leader and engineer at BBN Communications. The key success factor for S-QFD is flexibility. Charts should be changed to fit the project, the company, and the marketplace.[3]

Gathering voice of the marketplace data usually leads to a long list of features customers want in a product. These requirements must then be grouped and sorted. The outcome is a requirements list that must be limited to the critical requirements for the product. These critical requirements will be the basis for making trade-off decisions of time, cost, and resource allocation. Each of these major customer requirements must then be weighted according to its importance to the customer. Usually there are also requirements listed for internal company benefit such as backward compatibility, common form factors, regulatory agency requirements, and environmental requirements.

The final step in developing marketplace requirements is to rank the company's performance against those of the competition. This is done for each of the major competitors on a simple scale. A minus sign indicates being behind the competition, zeros indicate

Table V. Voice of the marketplace chart—competitive standing example for a switching product

Marketplace Requirements	Ranking	Competitive Assessment −	O	+
Fast processing of data	9		●	
Easy to use/maintain	1			●
High reliability	9		●	
Standards compliant	9	●		●
Small footprint	1			
Requires no special wiring/installation	1		●	
Transaction recognition and verification	6			
Security of data transfer	6	●		●
High availability	6		●	

Key

−	behind competitors
O	relative parity
+	competitive advantage

parity, where everyone is essentially equal, and a plus sign indicates a competitive advantage. Of course, the goal is to ensure that the product being developed will provide an advantage (+) over the competition for those requirements about which customers care most (9's). Table V illustrates the voice of the marketplace level of QFD in its completed form.

The key to successfully and efficiently using S-QFD to assist in meeting customer needs is to focus the analysis on the 20-30 items of primary importance. This is typically done in an iterative fashion, with each team member participating. Only by properly limiting the analysis can a firm apply the full advantage of S-QFD to a complex product. One Japanese laser printer company, for example, became so wrapped up in its QFD analysis that by the time the chart was completed a Taiwanese competitor had a product out and had captured market share. The Japanese company eventually scrapped its product and sourced laser printers from its Taiwanese competitor.

The next action in an S-QFD analysis is to develop technical interpretations or responses of each marketplace requirement. This will translate voice of the marketplace requirements to actionable

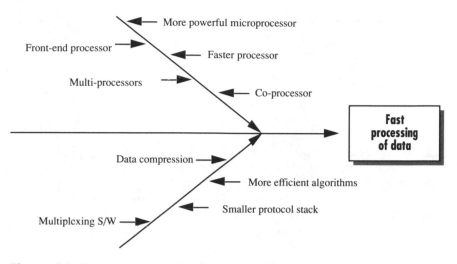

Figure 31. Interpreting marketplace requirements.

engineering tasks. It is at this stage in the process that S-QFD adds the most value to new product development. Here S-QFD assists the development team in conducting and documenting trade-off decisions in an organized manner. It also acts as a documentation trail so critical decisions can always be traced.

To translate marketplace requirements into actionable engineering or design activities, each requirement is looked at in a fresh manner. It's important that the team not try to satisfy requirements by using the same approaches the company has used in the past. This limits creativity and may eliminate new ideas for implementing functionality better and at lower cost. To do this, a fishbone chart, can be created for each requirement, such as the one shown in Figure 31.

Next the technical approaches are also narrowed in an iterative manner to focus on those of primary importance. This is done by estimating the time to complete each approach, the design cost associated with the alternative, the material or manufacturing cost of the alternative, the degree of difficulty, and the company's experience with the specific approach. Once each marketplace requirement has been technically interpreted, the requirements and technical approaches are plotted on an *X-Y* axis and correlations are investigated. Figure 32 highlights a simple QFD correlation matrix for conducting product trade-offs.

Key:
- ++ Strong positive correlation
- +   Positive correlation
- =   Strong negative correlation
- −   Negative correlation

Marketplace Requirements	Ranking	More powerful processor	Multiprocessors	Lower part count	Redundant hardware	MIL 2167A	Unix	S/W encryption	Message polling
Fast processing of data	9	++	++	−	−	+	−	−	−
High reliability	9	−	=	++	=	+	+	−	
Standards compliant	9					+	++		−
Security of data transfer	6						−	++	+
Transaction recognition verification	6						−		++
High availability	6				++	+	−		+

Figure 32. Correlation matrix.

The correlation matrix is used to ensure that each marketplace requirement has an associated technical approach. This keeps critical marketplace requirements in the forefront of the designer's thinking. It also helps to make sure key requirements are not overlooked.

Another value of the correlation matrix is that it makes certain that every technical action has an associated marketplace requirement. This prevents engineers from overdesigning the product and thus making it too complex and costly. In reality, analyzing the S-QFD correlation matrix should give both engineers and marketing people new ideas as alternatives are brought to light in an interactive manner with the entire Core Team participating.

S-QFD analysis can be continued beyond this point to understand the trade-offs of component selection, manufacturing process development, and so on. However, we have found that the main benefit lies in understanding marketplace requirements, developing alternatives, and conducting trade-off analysis through the development of the correlation matrix.

Design for Excellence (DFE)

The three most important new product factors from the customer's standpoint are quality, cost, and delivery. New product quality means a consistently good product with high reliability. Customers would like to know when they purchase the product that they don't have to worry about it working properly. High quality is expected. The quality of a new product depends heavily on the product's design.

Product cost depends quite heavily on the materials and manufacturability of the design. All too often we see products canceled before production because their cost is so high that the price would be unbearable. Considering cost as a design objective is critical for acceptance by the customer.

Finally, customers want their new products on time, every time. Today few companies can get by on the old technique of announcing that their new product will be available next quarter only to slip the introduction another six months. Ongoing delivery depends heavily on the parts and assembly processes specified by the product's design.

Managing these factors is the goal of design for excellence. Design for excellence means incorporating considerations other than pure product performance into the product design. This is done ultimately to lower the life-cycle cost of the product and therefore increase profitability. Some of the typical design considerations are

- *assembly*—making the product easier to assemble, thereby reducing cycle-time during production
- *manufacturability*—maximizing ease of manufacture by minimizing complexity through part count reduction
- *testability*—designing the product so that it can be effectively and efficiently tested
- *serviceability*—minimizing the occurrences of service calls and downtime per call
- *international*—designing for international roll-out
- *green*—designing environmentally conscious products

Each of these design considerations can be achieved by applying specific techniques. Some of the more successful techniques illustrate the benefits.

Design for assembly

Design for assembly (DFA) focuses on simplifying the assembly process, which ultimately reduces manufacturing time and improves product quality. This means designing the product so that its assembly is as foolproof as possible, because every bit of handling during the assembly process has the potential to introduce errors and variation.

The entire fabrication, subassembly, and assembly process must be as clear as possible. Components should be designed so that they can only be assembled in one way. Cutouts, notches, asymmetrical holes, and stops are some of the ways to foolproof the assembly process by design.

Specific elements of design for assembly typically include

- involving manufacturing and manufacturing engineering early in the design process
- avoiding tight tolerances
- being careful of tolerance stack-up on connecting parts
- designing part orientation to minimize handling
- avoiding using parts that can become tangled, wedged, or disoriented
- incorporating symmetry, low center for gravity, guide surfaces, easily identifiable features, and points for pickup and handling in part design
- considering the movement patterns of people or machines assembling the product and making them as simple as possible
- designing product and process concurrently
- striving for uni-axis assembly
- making adjustments easy and foolproof or eliminating them entirely

Design for manufacturability

Design for Manufacturability (DFM) seeks to maximize ease of manufacture by simplifying the design through part count reduction. Reducing the number of parts is important. Each part in a product means an opportunity to introduce defects and assembly errors. As part counts are reduced, the probability for a

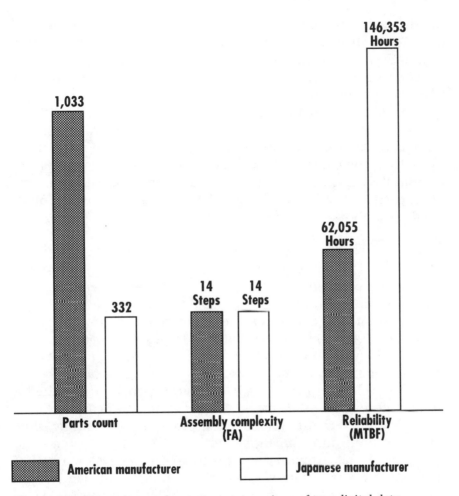

Figure 33. Measuring performance—comparison of two digital data communications products.

high quality product increases exponentially. Fewer parts also mean higher reliability, lower life-cycle costs, less design engineering labor (including less redesign), and less purchasing, stores, and quality assurance labor, as well as less floor space.

A systems company received a rude awakening on the need for DFM recently. A Japanese competitor came into the market with the same features and performance as its current, top-of-the-line product but with a reduced part count (see Figure 33). The American company had to quickly redesign its product to be cost competitive with the Japanese product. Fortunately, it was able to complete a DFM analysis and greatly improve its product before losing too much market share.

Cost reduction is another major reason to institute design for manufacturability. The cost of the part is obviously zero if it's eliminated but so are the associated costs of purchasing, stocking, and servicing that part. To determine the theoretical minimum number of parts required in a new design, ask the following questions: Does the part move relative to all other moving parts? Does it absolutely have to be made of a different material from the other parts? Does the part have to be different to allow for product disassembly?

Design for testability

The goal of design for testability (DFT) is to design a product so that the necessary tests can be efficiently generated and completed in the shortest amount of time. The testability of a design is indicated by the percentage of functionality covered by test nodes, but 100% coverage is usually an impossible goal. The effectiveness of trying to write additional test vectors is limited to the size and complexity of the product.

Test development has always been an expensive headache for product development teams. As designs increase in complexity, it can be expected that developing test programs will require more and more of the development budget and schedule. For some companies, it can take from six months to a year to develop an effective test program that will test the product sufficiently. The alternative—inadequate test coverage—can lead to dissatisfied customers and a product or company with a tarnished industry image. Because of this, design for testability is becoming increasingly important.

Also included in this is the concept of loosely coupled designs, where modules can be effectively tested in isolation and only a few tests need to be done to check the integration of the modules. In tightly coupled designs, many interactions have to be tested and a hierarchical approach cannot be taken. Also, tightly coupled designs tend to have many more combinations and paths to test, making comprehensive testing lengthy or impossible. An example is a recent TV software development where the use of a loosely coupled design reduced the test cycle time from two to three days to two to three hours.

Specific elements of design for testability typically include

- calculating test coverage and timing requirements
- including test engineers in the up-front, architectural stages of design
- employing built-in test components
- scanning testing
- partitioning circuitry for maximum effectiveness
- designing test point access
- designing component access
- designing failure mode indicators
- balancing available test equipment with design considerations
- understanding the acceptable failure rate and time-to-repair
- developing manufacturing-compatible test vectors
- designing tools that incorporate test support

Design for serviceability

Design for serviceability (DFS) means considering during the design cycle how the product will be serviced in the field. For low-cost products design for serviceability can be as simple as determining the cost of repair versus the cost of total replacement. For larger and more expensive products, however, serviceability is an important issue. Customers obviously don't want products that break down. Recognizing that this does happen though, if something does go wrong they want their systems up and running as fast as possible.

Some companies are incorporating diagnostic capabilities into their designs. Digital Equipment Corporation, for example, has spent hundreds of millions of dollars in artificial intelligence systems for diagnostics. Theoretically, these systems are so advanced that they can predict when a specific part of a customer's system is going to break down, order a replacement part, and get it in the customer's hands before the actual failure occurs.

DFS essentially means designing a product that can be readily serviced in the field in the smallest amount of time. Some of the specific elements of DFS typically include

- designing failure mode indication
- designing remote diagnostics
- considering diagnostic coverage and reporting

- determining field replaceable unit requirements
- minimizing time to repair
- increasing mean time between service calls
- designing hot pluggable servicing
- designing ease of disassembly

Design for international

Design for international (DFI) seeks to manage the design process in such a way that the product can be quickly adapted to each particular country or market it is sold into with the least amount of work. Minimizing the cost of international customization is what design for international is all about. DFI brings some unique characteristics to bear for technical, marketing, and development people. These characteristics include:

- varying standards from country to country
- different power requirements
- homologation issues
- diverse safety and environmental standards
- user interfaces that must appeal to different cultural norms
- language barriers and other communication difficulties

Figure Table VI highlights just a few of the various international standards that must be considered when designing for international.

One of the best examples of DFI is the Xerox 5100 copier. Introduced in 1990, the 5100 was the first jointly developed product, a collaboration between Fuji Xerox of Japan and Xerox Corporation engineers. The requirements for a successful copier product in Japan differ greatly from those in the United States. For example, paper is lighter weight and has a smoother finish, Kanji characters are much more complex and intricate, and the use of blue pencil lead is common. In the past, these factors meant that unique products had to be developed for each market. This, of course, led to each of these products being reengineered to fit the needs of other markets.

By employing DFI considerations, Xerox designed the 5100 series concurrently from concept to delivery. Input for the design was collected from customer groups in the United States, Europe, and Japan. The 5100 was introduced to the Japanese market in November 1990 and in the United States in February 1991. It was the

Table VI.   Selected international product standards

Country	Design standards
Germany	MedGV 14.01.85
Hungary	The Common Market (IEC) standard
India	ISMS 8519, 9858 616,9080
Netherlands	The Common Market (EEC) standard
Norway	IEC 601-1
Poland	The German DIN standard
Romania	The Common Market (EEC) standard
Saudi Arabia	SASO and British standards
Spain	German standards
Sweden	IEC 601-1
Syria	IEC standards

fastest global roll-out for any new product yet at Xerox. This design for international approach saved Xerox more than $10 million in development costs.

Design for green

Design for green (DFG) considers the design of the product (and the manufacturing process) from an environmental standpoint. Many companies are becoming increasingly aware of the impact of their products and associated manufacturing processes on the environment. Design for green seeks to reduce pollutants from the manufacturing process by eliminating hazardous by-products or shifting to benign by-products. DFG also strives to minimize the environmental impact of the product after its useful life through recyclability or allowing the product to safely decompose.

Some companies have made considerable DFG progress. Carrier Corporation spent $500,000 in 1988 to remove toxic lubricants from its manufacturing process, resulting in an annual production savings of $1.2 million by avoiding hazardous waste disposal costs. AT&T removed an ozone-depleting compound from its circuit board manufacturing process and saved $3 million annually. Polaroid recently eliminated mercury from its batteries, making its production environment safer and protecting the environment after the consumer throws away the battery.

As demonstrated by these examples, not only is DFG environmentally conscious, but often it can also lower manufacturing costs by eliminated the hidden costs associated with health problems and hazardous waste handling and disposal. Health claims are tremendous for miners with black lung disease and for people who had long-term exposure to asbestos. The same problems may confront the electronics industry because of the many hazardous chemicals used, for example, chemical exposure in the manufacture of printed circuit boards. DFG also minimizes the need for hazardous waste disposal, the costs of which continue to rise as waste sites fill and the public becomes alarmed, and thus government regulation grows.

DFG considers many factors throughout the development process, including

- Assuring ease of product disassembly for subassemblies, components, and base materials for eventual recycling or separation for hazardous and nonhazardous disposal. For example, plan for reuse of as many subassemblies as possible; make the product rechargeable instead of requiring disposable batteries; use single material subassemblies using single-plastic resins; use thermoplastic resins that can be recycled instead of thermosets; and don't permanently encase batteries in a product.
- Avoiding toxic substances wherever possible, both in manufacturing and disposal of the product. For example, limit the use of printing inks that contain heavy metals; if batteries are used in the design, specify mercury-free carbonized zinc or mercury-reduced zinclair batteries.

- Minimizing wasted materials used in packing and shipping or searching for environmentally friendly alternatives
- Including information with the product to educate consumers about the potential environmental impact of improper disposal of the product and encouraging responsible actions

User-Oriented Design

One of the challenges in the design of today's electronic products is allowing the user to take full advantage of the power and features possible with the advances in microprocessors and software. How many times have we encountered a VCR with the clock flashing "12:00" incessantly? How many of us have sat down with an IBM PC (before Windows 3.0) and tried to remember the arcane commands needed to manipulate files? These are just two of a myriad of occasions when product design has not been user oriented.

User-oriented design focuses on how the user interacts with the product (that is, user interface). This is especially critical as products grow in terms of complexity and capability. User-oriented design includes all the ways people can interact with a product:

- operational—the way the product is used every day
- installation—the time from receiving the box until the product is fully operational
- documentation—clearly and simply describing technical functions
- user training—quickly and painlessly learning how to use the product
- customer repair—allowing the user to easily diagnose and repair the product
- service—responsive and efficient

User-oriented design is becoming increasingly important as products grow in complexity. Software companies in particular find that user-oriented design pays off in terms of quicker market acceptance, leading to more customers.

Several factors driving user-oriented design include compatibility with other products (including those of the competitor), increasingly comprehensive industry standards (formal and de facto), and the transition from technically knowledgeable customers to those who desire "plug and play." In other words, today's customers don't care about the technical details of the product; they simply want it to work.

Much has been done in recent years in terms of standardization in the electronics industry. This has increased the need for user-oriented design as users demand compliance with formal and de facto standards. For example, if a personal computer manufacturer designed a system with a four inch diskette, few would purchase it as it is not in line with the de facto standards for diskettes.

The last major factor driving the need for user-oriented design is the user. Customers are no longer interested in changing components, swapping out circuit boards, or writing machine instruction code. Today's customers want to plug in a product and forget about the details of what makes it work. In fact, companies have even differentiated themselves on making products extremely easy for the user to interface with.

One of the best examples of user-oriented design is the Apple Macintosh computer, which has always been differentiated by its user friendliness. That its product margins are among the highest in the industry is no coincidence. Introduced in the mid 1980s, the Mac is still the easiest computer to use, without any fundamental design changes. Installation consists of plugging in the unit and switching it on, and instantly the user is in the Mac's "desktop." Arcane operating system commands are replaced by intuitively understandable icons. A mouse allows the user to move naturally around the screen instead of being confined by directional keys. All application programs have the same look and feel (pull-down menus, scroll bars, common key words), so that if the user has learned one program, learning others is simple. In the past few years all major computer and software manufacturers have attempted to duplicate the Mac's ease-of-use, which has set the de facto industry standard for graphical user interface.

User-oriented design is impacted by many functional areas—electrical, software, mechanical, packaging, documentation, and service. It has a few basic rules that should be considered early in development:

- Map the actions of users to their desired results in product response.
- Provide clear and consistent feedback to the user on results of each action.
- Make desirable actions visible and easy to understand.
- If an action is being performed incorrectly, clearly warn the user.
- Make detrimental actions invisible or difficult to do.
- Assure that the design is robust so that a mistake by the user is easily recoverable and does not result in major damage.

Design Technique Timing

Even though design for excellence techniques are powerful, their effectiveness relies on correct placement within the structured development process as shown in Figure 34.

- S-QFD takes customer input (Phase 0) and translates it into technical specifications (Phase I), then converts it into product design (Phase II), with the effectiveness of S-QFD diminishing greatly after detailed design has begun.
- With user interface often integral to the product concept, user-oriented design is undertaken early in development.
- International design considerations often impact the fundamentals of a product's design; therefore, design for international must begin before product specifications are finalized.
- Environmental considerations lead to design for green decisions affecting the basic materials and configuration of the product determined during Phase I.
- Design for assembly, manufacturability, and serviceability can only start when rough specifications are in place, thus allowing trade-offs to be made between specific aspects of the product's design.
- Design for testability is last, applied later in development, when the design is sufficiently complete to determine, and thus optimize, specific testing requirements.

Ultimately, these techniques should be seamlessly integrated

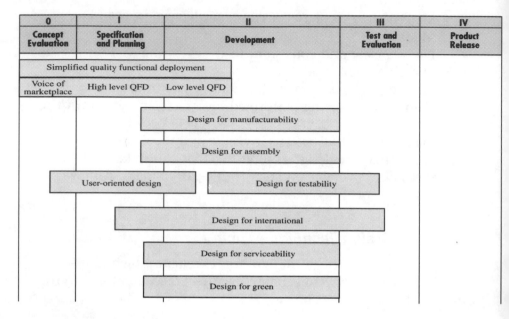

Figure 34. Design technique positioning within the structured development process.

into a company's PACE guidelines. Development guidelines should prompt the cross-functional reviews and interactions required to successfully use design techniques.

Automated Tools for Product Development

Once properly structured, the product development process can benefit greatly from the implementation of automated product development tools. These tools can accelerate and in some cases completely eliminate development tasks. A wide range of development tools can accelerate product development activities. For the sake of convenience in illustrating how they apply, we have used four categories: design tools, simulation tools, development tools, and project management and execution tools.

Design Tools

Automated design tools can play an important role in accelerating the early tasks of the product design process. They generally focus on the engineering or behavioral aspects of how the product or subsystem will function based on key inputs and expected outputs. By allowing engineers to quickly conduct "what-ifs" or a scenario analysis of desired functionality, they reduce the time required to determine the optimal design alternative. This capability also allows an engineer to test the limits of various design approaches on an automated design workstation before delving into the next layer of design. Examining several types of design tools illustrates these benefits.

Electrical design tools

Electrical design tools translate a design specification to an output package for circuit board development. Design tools can be applied to most of the tasks in the hardware design process. They are valuable for completing design specifications, controlling documentation, performing behavioral level modeling, analyzing part selection, creating schematics, simulating the design, developing net lists, and generating parts lists.

Automating these tools can save a significant amount of time. Additionally, the automated process can avoid many typical errors that impact later steps in the process.

Computer-aided software engineering

Computer-aided software engineering (CASE) tools facilitate applying engineering work methods to the process of developing software. Simply put, CASE tools are automated tools for the planning, analysis, and design of software. They eliminate many of the lower-level, mundane tasks (such as data base definition or screen generation), allowing people to focus on software design before coding.

CASE hides much of this lower-level detail from the user within its own set of generated routines. Doing this allows designers to concentrate on what they want to do instead of the details of how to do it. Thus, CASE allows software professionals to spend more time ensuring that requirements are clearly established and that the design of the system is approached properly instead of jumping into the coding task.

Mechanical design tools

Mechanical design tools are becoming increasingly important in such industries as consumer electronics, where the look of a product tends to change every 6–12 months. These tools can truly speed up the mechanical design process. Every type of design can be modularized and stored in a mechanical design component library. When developing a new product, the mechanical or industrial design engineer can then pull the desired modules out of the data base and modify them for a new product, rather than start from scratch.

The development of design tools for mechanical and industrial design has lagged that of electrical design tools by eight to ten years. Recently, however, as a result of the increasing power of workstations and personal computers, mechanical design tools have made important advances. They are no longer just two-dimensional electronic drafting boards.

Some tools even have the capability to create the mold patterns for the product. These then can be electronically transferred to the tooling vendor's system for review and modification during the tooling development cycle.

Simulation Tools

Designers simulate the mechanical or electrical portion of a design to analyze and evaluate the operational characteristics of the design to see if it will function as desired. Design tools conduct simulation by executing a software model that represents the specific product subsystem to be built.

Simulation shortens the design cycle by quickly verifying that a particular design approach is feasible. Simulating the design also tends to reduce the need for extensive prototyping, lowers test programming time, and reduces debugging time at hardware/software integration testing.

The design of an electronic product can be simulated at many levels: component, circuit, board, or system. Today most companies can simulate their electrical designs to the printed circuit board level, although a few very large companies have developed the ability to simulate the functionality of highly complex systems. Most companies, however, cannot afford the hardware and complex software programs to simulate at the systems level.

One data communications manufacturer first employed simulation tools early in 1991. It found that an experienced user was able to eliminate one prototype cycle, thus saving 12 weeks of design time. In addition, simulation also allowed users to routinely shave eight to ten weeks off of design verification time.

Development Tools

Automated development tools are used to translate a high-level design into an output file for fabrication. These tools quickly complete some of the mundane and time-intensive tasks of developing a new product and therefore reduce development time. This can be illustrated by looking at two types of development tools in use today.

Integrated-circuit or printed-circuit-board development tools

Integrated-circuit or printed-circuit-board development tools are typically used by a separate CAD department downstream from the electrical-design engineers. The input for these tools is the output package from design engineering tools and includes schematics, a netlist, and logic block diagrams. Development tools are used to turn this information into a completed integrated circuit (IC) or printed-circuit-board development file for fabrication.

These development tools automate the placement of components on the circuit board or substrate, then route the interconnections between the components themselves and the input/output connections on the board or chip. These tools are also used to conduct analysis of power consumption and thermal tolerance of the components and associated circuity to avoid problems with the design. Automating this step can cut weeks from a design cycle time and reduce errors. Many also incorporate design rule checkers to prevent users from inadvertently designing a product that won't function, and some also include manufacturability considerations for ease of manufacture.

Rapid prototyping

Rapid prototyping is one of the fastest growing design-tool areas. Systems have recently been developed that can create a physical prototype within hours or a couple of days (based on a part's size and complexity). Ordinarily this process could take many weeks or even months.

Rapid-prototyping tools also give designers a quick method of seeing and handling a part that is closely approximate to the final product. These rapid prototypes can be used for many advantages, for example, to

- debug early designs
- eliminate more expensive early prototypes
- check form and fit of mating parts
- test air and liquid flow, thermal, stiffness, and mechanical properties
- model hard-to-visualize sections of the design
- spotlight dimensional errors
- demonstrate manufacturability problems
- test customer reaction to new industrial designs

Project Management and Execution Tools

Automated tools can also assist in improving project management and execution. Properly used they can accelerate product development even more. Typical of such tools are those used for project scheduling, new-product financial analysis, video conferencing, and groupware.

Project scheduling tools
Project scheduling tools automate project planning and tracking. More than one hundred project scheduling software packages are available on the market today. They can relieve the Core Team from the manual process of keeping track of tasks and activities; especially helpful can be the generation of Gantt-type charts. Many of these tools can perform project scheduling in a layered fashion, where individual schedules can be created for elements of the design and then rolled-up into an overall schedule. Some can provide an overall vision chart of the entire project.

Project-scheduling tools are not a blueprint for project management. We find this to be a common mistake. Typically this happens when a project team is not given any guidance on how to manage projects. They provide project-management software that automates many techniques and manage their project without deciding which techniques are most appropriate.

Caution should be used when applying such tools as PERT and CPM. Methods that are suitable for managing physical tasks can slow down activities in product development, which requires developing information in a parallel fashion. As a project management technique, PERT can lead teams to develop tasks in too much detail, since hundreds of critical actions can take place in a week.

We find that the best tools for project scheduling are those that are easy to use from three perspectives. First, the tool should allow quick and easy to development of a project schedule. Second, it must be even easier to update or revise it. Finally, the ability to generate clean, easy-to-read reports is another very important feature.

New-product financial analysis tools

New-product financial analysis tools automate financial projections. In the early phases of product development, projecting the expected sales and financial analysis is a critical activity of the Core Team. With the popularity of PC-based spreadsheet tools, this task is now much easier. To be a truly effective tool, however, this needs to go one step further to the use of standard templates for new product planning and financial analysis.

In our experience, we have seen many project teams design their formats for this financial analysis. They spend more time putting together the worksheet than they do in validating their assumptions. As a result, the output looks nice, but the input was not thought through. Additionally, when this is presented to the PAC, the formats and analysis vary from project to project, making the PAC's job more difficult. The solution is to standardize this tool using a template.

Video conferencing

Video conferencing is a project management tool that is being increasingly accepted by product development teams that are geographically dispersed. One telecommunications company, for example, has marketing on the East Coast, R&D in California, a circuit-board manufacturing plant in Taiwan, and systems assembly in Mexico. Running a weekly Core Team meeting would be impossible or prohibitively expensive. With the use of video conferencing, the company is able to conduct meetings effectively in what approximates a real situation.

Video conferencing tools allow you to see the people you are meeting with even though they may be located in another state or country. This capability is a great improvement over teleconferencing, which is limited to audio. With video conferencing the Core Team can work on line to solve problems, manage the schedule, conduct design or documentation reviews, and improve communications among functions.

Groupware

Groupware tools are still in their infancy, but look for the number of applications and vendors to grow rapidly in the 1990s. Groupware tools allow members of a work group, such as a Core Team, to work on or edit the same document in parallel. For example, if a team is working on a functional specification or product development plan, all team members can generate sections of it and make edits concurrently. Some groupware tools have voice-note annotation so that while a person is making revisions, he or she can listen to inserted audio comments, questions, or advice from team members who are concurrently involved in creating it.

Common Problems in Implementing Automated Development Tools

To fully take advantage of what design tools have to offer, it is important to avoid some common traps into which many companies fall. Most of these problems can be avoided through careful planning and requirements definition before the tools are implemented.

The most common mistake in our experience has been to attempt to implement design tools without first structuring the product development process. The result of this is the ability to execute a very inefficient process faster, thus compounding inefficiencies.

Many managers have unrealistic expectations of what tools can accomplish. A learning curve is associated with any design tool, and some tools take much longer to learn than others. One systems company vice president didn't understand this. His design engineers became extremely frustrated at his demands to get the new design done in half the time because he had spent tens of thousands of dollars investing in electrical design tools. The lead engineer told us "he thinks that there's three buttons on the workstation. Press button one and the design is complete, press button two and we have six-sigma quality, then press button three and we beat the schedule." If only it were that easy.

Not understanding the supporting infrastructure required to use design tools effectively is another major problem. Just uncrating a design tool and plugging it in won't give a company any advantage. The users have to be trained in the tool and all of its capabilities; maintenance and control procedures have to be established; libraries must be either purchased and installed or specifically created; and resources have to be trained or hired to manage the design tool implementation. Failure to consider these factors adequately will result in tools that are not used or used and no benefit is derived from purchasing them.

Lastly, maintaining the integrity of a tool's data base is critical to its adding value to the design process. Many companies make the mistake of treating this lightly. Typically what happens then is a multitude of components get added to the data base. Many are redundant, some are outright wrong, and few are correctly documented. This of course creates a distrust of the data base; in reaction, various design groups create their own data bases and libraries. It doesn't take long for the entire process to get out of hand.

Another typical problem is that companies in the past often procured new design tools to address a specific problem at the time such as circuit board layout or mechanical design. Until recently, many tools optimized one element of the design process and inadequately addressed others. Electrical design tool vendors, for example, have had either great behavioral-level modeling and simulation capabilities or good circuit-board placement and routing development abilities, but not both. This led to designers purchasing tools from one vendor and the CAD group selecting a different vendor. The problem then becomes how to integrate these tools to avoid manual manipulation of data.

Not selecting a common hardware platform has also been a major problem in the past. Before Unix became so prevalent in the industry, it was not uncommon to walk into a mid-sized corporation and find multiple hardware platforms in the design area. The problem here is that design tool applications typically could not be swapped back and forth to run on Sun, Apollo, IBM, DEC, and Hewlett Packard hardware.

Before spending scarce dollars on new design tools, consider some of the following key factors:

- Understand the most complex designs today and estimate maximum complexity for the future.
- Gather information about each of the top vendor's equipment. (We recommend avoiding smaller, less stable vendors, as there has been enormous turnover in the industry in recent years.)
- Create a cross-functional team of designers to review vendor promotional material and interview vendor technical applications support staff.
- Benchmark each of the vendor's tools using one of your most complex designs.
- Review each vendor in terms of tool performance, integration with present systems, training, and support.
- Don't purchase on initial cost alone. Consider life-cycle costs, including maintenance and training.

Summary

Used in the context of a structured product development process, design techniques and automated development tools can greatly improve product quality while reducing time to market. The following summarizes how this can be applied to the development process:

- QFD is a technique to make design trade-offs and translate customer requirements into new products.
- S-QFD is a simplified approach for complex products.
- Design for excellence groups techniques for incorporating operational considerations into product designs.
- Design tools focus on the front end of the process and typically operate at a high level.
- Simulation lets designers conduct "what if" scenarios to determine an optimal approach.
- Development tools are used to turn a concept into a detailed output package ready for fabrication.

- Common problems experienced in implementing design tools are covered.
- Tips for tool selection and implementation are given.

References

1. Yoji Akao, *Quality Function Deployment-QFD* (Productivity Press, Cambridge, Mass., 1990).
2. William E. Eureka and Nancy E. Ryan, *The Customer-Driven Company: Managerial Perspectives on QFD* (ASI Press, a division of American Supplier Institute, Inc., Dearborn, Michigan, 1988).
3. Peter Burrows, "In Search of the Perfect Product," *Electronic Business,* June 17, 1991, p. 73.

9

Cross-Project Management

When a company has only one product development project, everything revolves around that project. With multiple projects, however, comes the need for certain activities to be managed across all projects. Effective management of these activities across all projects creates the infrastructure necessary for projects to be most successful.

Product strategy and technology management, which were discussed in Chapters 6 and 7, help to initiate and define product development projects. In addition, other cross-project activities need to be managed. The specific activities vary by company, but there are five that are generally necessary in most cases (see Figure 35).

Resource scheduling is necessary to keep track of the resources, particularly people, that have been scheduled and when they are available to be scheduled on new projects. *Business systems interfaces* define how product development works as part of a total business system to support business planning, budgeting, financial reporting, and so on. *Portfolio management* enables a company to understand and manage the mix of projects that it has under development. *Product development process engineering* enables continuous improvement of the product development process, including the training necessary to develop and maintain skills across all projects. *Functional interfaces* define how various functional organizations support the Core Teams in their development efforts.

Resource Scheduling

The natural tendency is to schedule more development than can be completed. This is similar to the old theory of manufacturing that the best way to achieve productivity is to overload

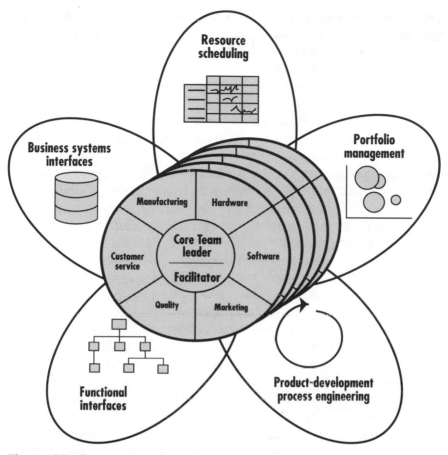

Figure 35. Resource scheduling.

the factory so that it is always working. With the advent of JIT, companies eventually found that it was output that mattered, not input. The same is true in product development. Overscheduling product development will only lead to inefficiency and delays. Stuffing more into the front end of the process in an attempt to get more out merely lengthens the cycle time of everything.

One electronic instrument manufacturer suffered from this re-source overloading problem. Having a strong willed CEO who liked to tinker with the engineering organization didn't help. When we reviewed the company's past projects we noticed that they took three to four times longer to complete than the compe-tition. Digging deeper we found that like most companies, this company allocated development resources on an annual budgeting basis. The CEO, however, constantly gave engineering people special small projects to work on. By April the annual budget was 150% allocated! The CEO couldn't understand why everything took so long. "A couple of guys in a garage could do it in a month" was his favorite saying. Upon asking people how many projects they had assigned to them, a typical response was 14-16! This was scheduling across projects assuming infinite capacity.

The PACE elements of Core Team organization, phase review decision making, and structured development will improve scheduling of individual projects. They will ensure that the best organization and resources are defined for each project, as well as enabling accurate and reliable schedules. In addition, they will provide the framework for proper decision making to establish priorities, but they will not prevent overscheduling of resources if the information is not available to functional managers and the PAC.

In another example, a small semiconductor manufacturer had many late development projects. Everyone seemed to be working very hard, yet products were not being developed on schedule. One manager calculated the development staff loading and found that the typical engineer was assigned to several projects and was scheduled to well over 200% capacity. Obviously, the development organization was overloaded and, as a result, all projects were slipping.

Resource scheduling can be implemented in different ways. It can be based on head count assigned to projects by month or done at a more detailed level such as man-days. It can be PC-based or part of a large integrated computer system. It can include collection of actual time as part of a project accounting system or simply be a scheduling and decision-making tool.

The role of resource scheduling is to provide the information on which resources—people, support functions, critical equipment, and so on—are committed and which are available. This enables Core Team leaders to see where there are resource constraints. The functional managers can understand how their resources are being assigned and see in the future what skills they need. The PAC can use this information to set priorities since it allows them to see what skills are about to become bottlenecks. If the bottlenecks are seen early, senior management can take proactive action to avoid them.

Core Team

The Core Team leader and the rest of the Core Team use resource scheduling to identify where there are resource constraints. By having this information available, we have found that the team can modify the schedule a little or redefine responsibilities so that the schedule is realistic for the resources available. They are also able to identify a critical need in the future so that there is enough time to hire a person with the skills needed or to find a contractor. Without this information, teams typically just define what they need and expect that they will be given the resources. Of course, when the resources don't materialize, the project falters. Unaware of the bottlenecks in advance, Core Teams have little flexibility to respond.

When a project is approved, the requested resources are assigned to the project team for the next phase. This means that they are not available for other projects. After Phase I approval, resources for phases beyond Phase II are usually allocated for completion of the project but not fully committed.

Resource scheduling also limits the people working on the project to those approved. Sometimes accounting practices encourage assignment to projects for budget allocation purposes or to use up available staff. In one company, manufacturing typically assigned 10–15 people to a project in order to allocate their costs, even though only one or two were needed.

The approved project schedule becomes the basis for commitment of resources to the project. The Core Team should work with functional management to change it as necessary. This usually happens when more time is required, there are trade-offs between projects, people leave the company, and so on.

Functional Managers

Functional managers use resource scheduling to understand how their staff is assigned to projects. The schedule should identify who is working on each project for future time periods. When new projects are being planned, this information shows when people are expected to be available.

Resource scheduling is also used to schedule activities other than product development such as training, technology development, and internal functional projects. It can also be used to allocate resources to ongoing activities such as customer support.

Resource scheduling also provides the information functional managers need to manage their own resources. They can see where there are expected shortages and the skills needed. This gives them time to hire or initiate the training necessary to prepare for upcoming needs. Typically this information will initially show that all functions need to hire more people. This is not usually the correct response; more likely, priorities need to be better established by the PAC.

PAC

The PAC uses resource scheduling to assure that the resources are available when it approves a project. If there is a shortage, the PAC can decide on the priority of the project being approved relative to projects previously approved. Resource scheduling also provides the information the PAC needs at the phase review to decide if there is a need to hire an additional person or contractor.

Another use of this information by the PAC and senior management is to see where there is an imbalance of skills within the company. With rapid changes in technology, most companies find that their skill mix is out of balance. Severe shortages develop in critical areas while excesses emerge in others. If the skills mix is unbalanced, the company will be limited by the most critical skill and be less productive.

When one company prepared its first realistic resource schedule, management saw a major imbalance of skills. To solve this the company eliminated 150 unneeded positions and added 50 in areas where there was a critical need. When combined with other changes, the company was able to develop twice as many products with fewer people.

Business Systems Interfaces

A number of business systems require information collected from all development projects. Interfaces to product development required to collect this information should be as efficient as possible so a high administrative burden can be avoided.

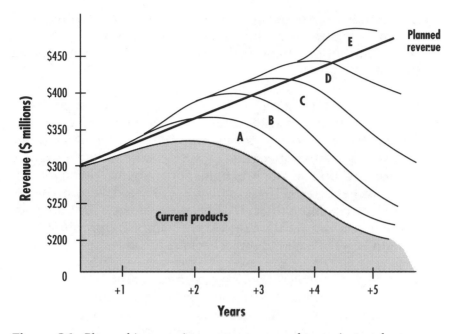

Figure 36. Planned increase in revenue compared to project under development.

Specific business systems vary by company, but a few examples illustrate the interfaces necessary to these systems:

1. *Business planning.* The term *business planning* is used here to describe planning for the next few years, typically a five-year period. The primary interface required is to link the planned increase in revenue to a roll up of the forecasts for individual product development efforts.

Figure 36 illustrates an example of business planning using a technique that layers forecasted revenue. The forecast for current products shows that sales are expected to decline over the next five years. This is typical in almost all companies. New products A, B, C, D, and E are expected to make up the difference and provide for growth. The forecasted revenues of these products are shown as layers on each other. The revenue projected for the next five years in the business plan is indicated on the chart, showing the margin for forecasting error.

In addition to revenue forecasting there may be other required inputs into business planning, such as manufacturing volumes and new distribution channels. These need to be accommodated as efficiently as possible.

2. *Budgeting.* Budgeting for the upcoming year is usually most efficient by function instead of project. This requires a link between functional budgets and product development resource plans. Exceptions that frequently cause problems are expenses such as tooling, outside purchases like software, prototype materials, and travel expenses. These expenses may need to be managed differently with a more direct link between projects and budgets. Annual budgets can be thought of as functional appropriations, but the funds get released to projects phase by phase, not annually.

3. *Project accounting.* Some companies maintain project accounting for development activities. The interface between development projects and project accounting should be as seamless as possible. Project accounting should collect costs using the same structure of phases, steps, and tasks. Budgets used in project accounting should be based on the resource schedule.

More companies however, are questioning the value of project accounting. They find the information frequently inaccurate and of little practical use. Typical is the company that had all development staff charge time to authorized projects. While the accounting staff that managed these data emphasized precision (for example: $129,200 engineering cost per man-year), the development staff had little discipline in how it charged this time. The resulting information was of little use. Now the company uses information from resource scheduling to make decisions.

4. *Quarterly reviews.* Most companies conduct monthly or quarterly reviews, particularly large multidivision companies. Typically, some section of this review deals with product development status. Such a review is most efficiently performed by building on what was already established during the Phase Review Process. In most cases status can be simply affirmed against schedule and goals with any changes or problems highlighted.

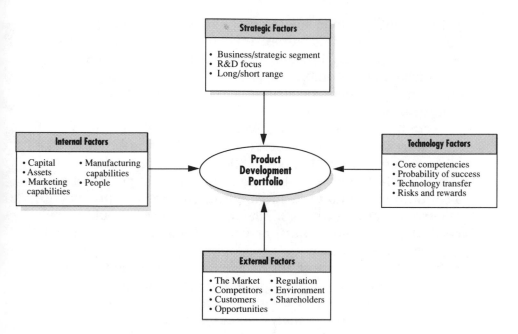

Figure 37. Portfolio management balances many factors.

These are examples of typical business processes where information across all projects needs to be included; there are frequently others. All are part of the infrastructure that requires cross-project interfaces.

Portfolio Management

Portfolio management involves managing the mix of product development projects so that it conforms to various strategies for technologies, markets, and business segments. It provides guidance to the PAC at phase reviews for project selection and resource allocation. As illustrated in Figure 37, portfolio management balances many factors by aiming at a balanced set of product development projects. Strategically it balances development by the business segment, R&D focus, and long- versus short-range impact. Too much emphasis, for example, on short-range product development could lead to long-term disadvantages.

Internally, portfolio management tries to balance the use of capital, assets, and capabilities. In many cases this balancing is needed to effectively implement the company's overall strategy. Too much emphasis on one capability and underutilization of another can cause internal constraints in one area and deterioration of the other.

Portfolio management also balances external factors. Even if one market segment has the best opportunities, it may not be wise to ignore customers and opportunities in other segments. Finally, technology factors need to be balanced. Core competencies need to be continually improved and applied. This requires product development that uses them. Similarly, the risk level should be balanced. High risk in all projects may lead overall to an unacceptable gamble for the company.

Portfolio management allows the PAC to manage the mix. It may, for example, approve funding of a project that provides balance to the portfolio over another with apparently better financials. The way portfolio analysis is implemented varies with the size of the company. In smaller companies it can be informal or even intuitive. In larger companies it needs to be a more formal analysis.

Product Development Process Engineering

Continuous improvement of the product development process is necessary to maintain its effectiveness and improve it to become world class. This requires ongoing attention to the process itself, including managing it as a process and planning for continuous improvement.

Typically a process engineering group is established with the assigned responsibility to manage the product development process when a process such as PACE is established. This group provides support and facilitation on the use of the process and modifies it as the needs change. When one project team finds a better way of performing a step, then this improvement can be implemented across all projects by the product development engineering group.

The process engineering group should develop an annual plan for improving the process. With this group members identify where the best opportunities are for improving the process along with the implementation plan for achieving them. They should also establish metrics for the product development process and regularly measure how the process is doing. The Codex division of Motorola has a process engineering group that regularly plans improvements to the process and measures results. Codex has been able to achieve a continuous improvement in time to market of 10–15% per year. The group has become a resource for functional managers to call upon to help solve problems with the process, benchmark it, and compare it to world-class companies.

Product development training is also required for all product development staff, including Core Team leaders, Core Team members, and other selected members to be full team. Additionally, technical training is necessary for most technically oriented development staff. These training requirements span all projects and should be managed separately, as is the process engineering responsibility.

Functional Interfaces

The implementation of PACE, particularly the Core Team project organization and Phase Review Process, creates some changes in the operation of various functional organizations. Functional organizations move more toward functional leadership by establishing guidelines, developing new tools, providing training, and defining functional strategy. Their objective is technical excellence, and their focus is to set the vision and technical direction. They relinquish the day-to-day product development tasks to the Core Team.

As the role of functional departments in product development changes, so does the way they need to operate relative to product development projects. This requires a clear definition of how each function interfaces to product development, including the following:

- How do the different departments within a function interact with the Core Team member?
- What is the role of the Core Team member regarding the function?
- How does a function gets involved at each phase?

- What guidelines, plans, and tools should be provided by the functional experts?

It is important that these be clearly defined as part of the infrastructure to support all product development projects. Without this definition, confusion will slow development efforts.

Summary

Cross-project management involves those activities that a company needs to manage across all projects or require an interface to all projects. Some examples of cross-project management include the following:

- Resource scheduling that keeps track of resources assigned to projects.
- Business-systems interfaces that relate product development activities to other processes.
- Portfolio management to balance many factors as part of project selection.
- Product development process engineering to manage continual improvement.
- Training to support all projects.
- Functional organization interfaces to define the required infrastructure to functional groups.

Implementation

10

Stages in the Evolution of the Product Development Process

New product development is one of the most intricate and critical processes of any company. We have stressed the process view of new product development throughout this book. Preceding chapters have described individual processes of the total process, such as the Core Team approach to project organization and the Phase Review Process. These processes, however, cannot be improved independently of one another. PACE integrates and balances improvements to each of the individual processes of new product development.

All companies—even those with long cycle times and a history of many troubled development projects—have a product development process in place, whether or not they recognize it as such. Although it's hard to change a process, even an ineffective one, PACE provides both a methodology and an approach for successfully making these changes. In Chapter 12 we'll talk about the challenges and rewards of implementation. The resolve to address all the major elements must be summoned in order to make the full process change. This is the challenging part. The rewarding part is this: once the improvements are made, they pay off and usually continue.

In this chapter we focus on the stages through which corporations evolve as they improve new product development. Each stage is a coherent process, with its own internal checks and balances, characteristics, and standards of performance. Understanding each stage is invaluable in determining what improvements should be made. This evolutionary framework is in our view difficult or impossible to short circuit. Companies rarely if ever skip a stage, because the discipline and mastery of each stage seems to be a prerequisite for advancing to the next one. Companies can, however, dramatically increase the speed and thoroughness with which this evolution proceeds. Understanding this framework can lead to earlier recognition of the opportunities for improvement and a realistic assessment of the effort required to make the step change.

Evolving toward Product And Cycle-time Excellence

There are four principal stages in the evolution of new product development (see Figure 38 and Table VII).

- *Stage 0. Incomplete new product development.* In Stage 0 certain necessary elements of a product development process are either missing or extremely weak. The failure of product development threatens the survival of the business or company.
- *Stage 1. Functional new product development.* Stage 1 is the classic stage during which product development responsibilities are distributed across strong functional organizations, and coordination takes place through hand-offs and internal contracts. Improvement is typically functionally focused.
- *Stage 2. Integrated new product development.* Stage 2 is marked by functional integration at many levels, from the Core Team to the Product Approval Committee. It is the first true step toward product and cycle-time excellence.
- *Stage 3. World class new product development.* Stage 3, achieved by the most successful product development organizations, is marked by a mix between functional (i.e., manufacturing) and business process (i.e., scheduling) excellence.

Companies go through these stages because of constraints on rates of change. Above all, corporations are bounded by one simple constraint: they can be truly superior in only a few attributes. Some companies are marked by functional excellence, others by excellence in their business processes. Excellence is built and maintained through consistency and focus, and the particular strengths of a given company are those imbedded in its culture, organization, and operations. These strengths are usually the ones

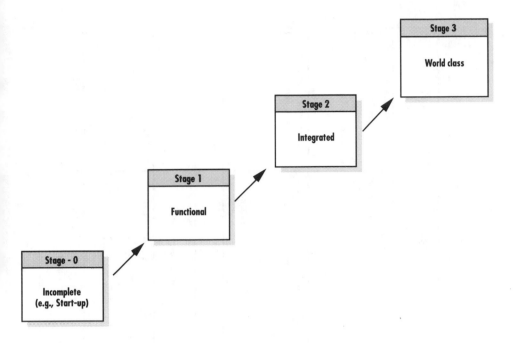

Figure 38. Typical stages in the evolution of product and cycle-time excellence.

that built the company and are most highly prized. This kind of consistency can be maintained only for a few key strengths.

Another constraining factor, we suspect, relates to the limitations of communication. Corporations have a limited capacity to absorb new messages. Today, people are often deluged with new information and changing trends.

How many corporations suffer from initiative overload? Where management has championed many new programs simultaneously (Malcolm Baldrige, ISO-9000, JIT, quality circles, QFD, customer focus, innovation, entrepreneuring, employee involvement, management by objectives, shareholder value creation, and so on) the organization often cannot absorb them all. Employees learn to pay them lip service and wait for the next program of the month. Management can drive only a very small number of initiatives at one time. Perhaps it can initiate a great many in sequence, but even this number is fairly limited.

Table VII. Characteristics in the stages of evolution toward product and cycle-time excellence

	Stage 0 Troubled	Stage 1 Functional	Stage 2 Integrated	Stage 3 World Class
Product development process	• Informal • Formal process not practiced or atrophied	• A process for each function with disparate steps, etc. Varying definitions abound	• One integrated process known to all and followed consistently	• Process among the best in the world and continuously improving • High rate of successful innovation or new product introduction
Project organization	• "Missiles and grenades over walls" • "Free for all"	• Strong functional walls/ boundaries • Internal "politics" are strong	• Dedicated cross-functional core teams • Good functional integration • Strong project management	• Experienced Core Teams • Capable of multilocation development
Management review process	• Focus is on release problems	• Monthly project reviews	• Event-based throughout the process	• Internalized as part of the culture
Strategic role	• Process failures threaten survival	• Process is detrimental to competitiveness	• Process permits parity with industry leaders	• Process as a source of competitive superiority • Strategies exploit process
Project managment	• No project planning or schedules done once then shelved	• Schedules exist in abundance, but are not integrated	• Teams use schedules and tools as keys for project success	• Scheduling linked to process improvement
Design tools	• None	• Some, but not integrated	• Integrated tools	• Completed EDA linked to factory and vendors
Design standard and techniques	• "We never do the same thing twice"	• Partial unrelated standards exist within areas of specialization	• In place and training available	• Continuously updated • Used as performance indicators

Product cost	• Not predictable	• Different estimate	• Product cost highly predictable	• Uses life-cycle cost models
Target setting	• Wishful thinking or none at all	• By edict ("you will complete this by...")	• Based on process norms (e.g., cycle-time guidelines)	• Based on world-class benchmarks
Product planning	• Not done or done opportunistically	• Done periodically • Often disconnected • Usually only 1-2 yrs. out	• A cross-functional responsibility • Focuses on product line strategy	• Highly integrated • Common vision
Technology planning	• None	• R&D responsibility • Tendency to ivory tower • Distinction between technology and product development not well maintained	• Long range • Distinction between technology and product development	• Long range and integrated • Product strategy • Strategic options identified
People management	• Random	• Functional kingdoms • Headcount important	• Teaming skills highly valued	• Everyone wants to work here
Customer involvement (QFD)	• None	• Marketing seen as surrogate for customer	• QFD and related techniques in some use	• Customer effectively integrated into process
Strategic vendor alliances	• None. Hostile relationship	• Critical components only; one-way street	• Seen as strengthening the process	• Integrated into process
Performance measurement	• None quantified. Information disguised	• Functional only • No process metrics	• Metrics used as management tool	• Consistent metrics • Regular external benchmarking
Time to market performance	• May be infinite	• Inconsistent & unpredictable	• 40-60% of Stage 1	• Best in industry and declining

Companies that are truly superior in one area or another tend to worry about maintaining that superiority. 3M, for example, is noted not only for its record of innovation, but also for the amount of time and attention it spends on self-assessment and keeping track of its innovation record. Not satisfied with being used so often in the business press as an example of good innovation practices, 3M periodically reviews those practices to check whether it is living up to its press, and the company maintains an extraordinary data base of project data that help it to understand which factors are predictors of project success.

The implication of so much cultural inertia is that moving from one stage to the next is a difficult process. Achieving these step improvements is the challenge of implementation, which we will discuss in Chapter 12. It is well worth the effort, however. As difficult as it may be for a company, it is probably as difficult for that company's competitors. Reaching a higher stage affords a sustainable advantage, and the achievement is hard to reverse. In fact, it is as difficult to undo a step improvement to Stages 2 or 3 as it is to make them in the first place.

Stage 0—Incomplete Product Development

Companies in Stage 0 have not yet achieved the ability to consistently develop new products. Their product development pipeline is clogged, and continuous survival may be a challenge. The root cause may be a functional weakness. For example, engineering may be strong, but manufacturing weak or nonexistent. Without stable functional performance, the product development process is unreliable. No self-sustaining process is in place.

Occasionally companies with Stage 1 development processes so burden those processes with unnecessary detail or neglect them so thoroughly that they collapse. Then informal processes must be relied upon. If these are lacking or never developed, companies can regress to Stage 0.

As can be seen in Table VII, the characteristics of companies at Stage 0 show an absence of any fundamental process. Everything is done informally or opportunistically. Performance is unreliable.

Companies in this stage have difficulty bringing successful products to market. If they do manage to release a marketable product, they're generally forced to turn to other companies to supplement their missing capabilities. For example, a biotechnology start-up built around the credentials of several academic founders might have to turn to an established pharmaceutical firm in order to take its product to market.

Some start-ups, by contrast, have all the characteristics of Stage 2 product development. This is especially true of highly successful and rapidly growing start-ups. These organizations so reflect the highly integrated vision of a few founders or key individuals, in touch with almost all the details of day-to-day business, that *de facto* functional integration occurs. In effect, these organizations have the Core Team and Product Approval Committee combined in the tightly knit group of key developers.

Often as such organizations grow, they find that duplicating their initial successes becomes much more difficult. The functions become more distinct. The founders have increasing difficulty staying in touch with all the details. Typically an influx of individuals from other organizations leads to new sets of expectations. Such organizations must usually go back to Stage 1 in order to develop and then return to Stage 2. If they understand this development cycle, these companies can make this transition happen much more quickly. If the founders understand that in Stage 2 they will be duplicating in a much more complex organization some of what they did instinctively in the start-up period, they can bring this process about much more easily.

Development performance in Stage 0 companies is generally not competitive. In fact, when mature organizations occasionally go back to this stage, they typically find that their development times are growing longer rather than shorter, and many of their interventions prove to be counterproductive. These organizations are also marked by many product failures or products brought to market that turn out to be unacceptable in terms of performance, quality, and/or cost.

Stage 1—Functional Product Development

Stage 1 is the most commonly found stage of product development processes. Companies in this stage tend to focus on strong functional skills, which in some isolated cases may be world class.

The product development process in Stage 1 companies is focused within, not across, functions. Linkages among the functions tend either not to be standardized or standardized in extremely formal and time-consuming ways. In Stage 1 functional new product development, there is a process in place, and it is often documented. The process documentation, where is exists, however, is often overelaborate. In some organizations such documentation can take up volumes. As a result, it is difficult to use and tends to fall into disuse. Some functional processes required in new product development may be lacking or *ad hoc* (that is, developed anew for each development project). People in the organization often see the relations between functions as contractual. More effort seems to be devoted to carefully defining the mutual responsibilities of the functions than to finding ways to streamlining their interactions. Over-the-wall activity is common since there are so many walls.

In these organizations responsibility for product development typically shifts at various points in the process from one function to another. Often marketing or product management is responsible in the earliest stage; occasionally it's R&D. Then responsibility shifts to engineering. After that it moves to manufacturing and product management or sales.

These transfer points are often points of great conflict and difficulty. They become interfunctional battlefields, especially when accepting the development over the wall includes accepting responsibility for problems that may not have been fixed earlier in the development process.

Organizations often try to improve this largely serial process by finding ways to move the wall. For example, some companies ask manufacturing engineers to take on some of the development engineers' responsibilities as a way of assuring that these activities are completed before ramp-up. In one organization the documentation group found itself creating the product functional specifications, which were only loosely produced during the development process and never frozen.

In Stage 1, project organization is a conspicuous weak point. The relative power of each function diminishes the power of project managers. Such organizations often have weak project managers or none at all. Project managers are often administrators, record keepers, or facilitators. We sometimes call such project managers "I, Claudius" project managers; they record the history of the project but don't powerfully influence its course. They keep the records while Rome burns.

Because authority and responsibility tend to reside more in the functions than in the development project team, issues of accountability are often quite unclear. When one looks at troubled development projects in Stage 1 companies, one sees a recurring pattern of shifting responsibility through the life of the project. Often decisions made by one function are undone by another. This form of project organization tends to work when time is not of the essence and where development projects go smoothly, but it tends to break down when there is stress. The greater allegiance of development team members to their function than to the overall business or project leads them to parochial decisions. When things go wrong, the functions tend to blame each other for problems. A clear symptom of this kind of organization is a paper trail throughout the project in which functions address each other. There are sharp memos full of statements such as "Marketing believes . . ." or "Engineering thinks . . ." or "Manufacturing feels. . . ."

The management decision making in Stage 1 organizations is often based on sign-off procedures. This is a time-consuming and politically charged activity. The sign-off decision can be pocket vetoed by any of the critical functions, and there is no urgency built into the procedure. Decisions are made when time permits.

In some cases sign-off requires that many levels in the organization's functional hierarchy be consulted and give their approval. This makes many of the signers potential disapprovers, but only the one at the top of the hierarchy is a truly authorized approver. When problems arise—for example, over differing visions of what a product should be—a sign-off process can grind to a halt. In disciplined organizations this results in delay. In more free-form organizations, this leads to deferred resolution of the open issue. Developers go forward without all the signatures required and hope for the best. If problems arise, those who withheld their signatures tend to disavow the project.

Highly functional organizations are often marked by a lack of consistency in scheduling within and across projects. Although schedules typically exist in abundance, they are often not integrated in a way that allows for master scheduling of development projects. Because the responsibility for the project tends to shift, the schedules often cover only parts of the development project. Those making these partial schedules may not feel ownership of the initial schedule set at the project outset. Such schedules tend to lack integrity and are not regularly updated or reconciled; consequently performance to schedule may not be reported to management on a timely basis. When we ask developers in Stage 1 organizations to show us their project schedules, the common answer is, "Which one do you want to see?"

The functional mode of new-product development also deals a blow to concurrent engineering. Because development in this stage tends to suboptimize on the needs of each function's contribution, there is little incentive for parallelism or concurrent engineering. The downstream functions such as manufacturing and service tend not to get involved in a project until quite late or when the ball is in their court. Because it is so difficult and costly to make changes in a development project in later stages, this absence of parallelism produces both costs overruns and time delays.

In functional Stage 1, considerable energy is devoted to internal issues, often to the detriment of objective external focus. This often manifests itself in setting targets for development. The targets for an individual development project in terms of cost, schedule, or quality tend to be based more on objectives than cycle-time guidelines. Often these targets are the result of negotiations between the functions, such as product functional specification resulting from negotiations between marketing, R&D, or engineering and manufacturing. In the better versions of this process, the negotiations take place early; more commonly the targets are renegotiated at the transfer points between functions.

Senior management commonly loses patience with the parochial process and loses confidence in the representations made by the individual functions. Senior managers often believe that schedules presented to them are padded and targets set at levels that are not challenging enough. They often respond by imposing new targets. Schedules are set based on rules of thumb such as cutting in half whatever R&D says or on some perception of when the market window will be open. Developers tend to ignore or become demoralized by such imposed targets. Some developers even keep two schedules, one that they show to management and the real one that they use to guide project activities. All this leads to lack of correlation between targets established at the outset of projects and actual performance.

Functional Stage 1 organization also makes product line planning difficult. Because responsibility for development is split between functions, the long-range planning of strategists or marketers takes on a certain unreality. After all, they often do not control what will go into the next product. In practice, the time horizon for effective planning tends to be quite short. The focus is on the next product, not the product as part of a product line. This can lead to an opportunistic, nonstrategic selection process.

A similar problem occurs in basic technology development. The essential separation of the functions may lead to R&D investments in technologies that may not be applied in future products.

To summarize Stage 1, functionally oriented new product development forms on the separate contributions of each function. Where time is not an issue, this process has the advantage of a slow and careful exercise of each function's skills. Where time is of the essence, this process tends to deliver new products very late. Typically the time to market of Stage 1 companies is more than twice that of benchmark world-class competition and approximately twice that of companies in Stage 2, or the integrated stage.

Stage 2—Integrated Product Development

Once companies have advanced from the purely functional Stage 1 and overcome the functional divisions, they enter Stage 2, or integrated product development. The chief characteristic of this stage is the effective integration of all functions involved in new product development throughout the process. Teams are cross-functional. Management review and decision making are cross-functional. The structured development process is cross-functional. In this stage, the product development process is practiced by most of the organization and is used consistently on all major product development projects. Companies in this stage put more focus on the project.

The role of the functions in Stage 2 development is as critical as ever, but it is clearly distinguished from the responsibility for developing individual products. Functions now have the principal responsibility of maintaining and deepening their skills and providing the necessary resources for individual development projects. In Stage 2 organizations, the functional boundaries are much less rigid than in Stage 1. In the best Stage 2 organizations, development teams have dedicated full-time members, often operating within the Core Team model.

These teams have representatives of all the critical functions and are made up of individuals highly committed to the project. Core Team members represent their function in the Core Team. They may go back to the functional hierarchy to test the validity of certain decisions and to return with full commitment of the function. They are not hampered by that hierarchy, however, nor is their principal role to guard the interest of their function in the Core Team deliberations.

In Stage 2 organizations project managers have considerable influence and prestige, and they maintain the balance between the importance of projects and the importance of the functions. They are fully capable of resolving major issues and conflicts. They are empowered to go anywhere in the organization to work on project-specific problems, and they stand as equals with their functional counterparts.

Stage 2 organizations achieve integration at many levels. Clearly they do so at the project level through effective Core Teams. They also do so at the management review level. Through mechanisms such as the Product Approval Committee (PAC), they achieve integrated decision making. In these organizations the decision-making process is not a sign-off process but more typically an action-oriented Phase Review Process. These are not *pro forma* status reviews but true decision points. Integrated teams of managers representing general management and all the major functions whose resources are drawn upon to develop new products will meet regularly to review the progress of projects. These management teams are well integrated and quite effective. Typically they make decisions at the time of the phase review, including decisions about the attractiveness of individual projects and their funding and resourcing.

Because these integrated management teams include both those with responsibility for setting the strategic course of the business and those who control the major resource pools, there is much less likelihood of decision making at cross purposes. A decision to go with the project is also a decision to commit resources to it. This integration at several levels—the senior-management level and the Core Team level—and effective communication through the Phase Review Process lead to great consistency in decision making.

Whereas scheduling was largely a politically negotiated or imposed process in Stage 1, in Stage 2 scheduling is based on cycle-time guidelines. These guidelines exist for each step of the process and typically vary with the characteristics of the projects, such as complexity and the degree of reliance on new technology. Cycle-time guidelines are in effect standard costing for time. They break the estimating process down to logical components (steps) and reflect variability due to such factors as product complexity or degree of innovation required. They improve setting a project schedule by focusing on the *content* of development, not on evaluations of the motives of those preparing the schedules. A company in Stage 2 rationally schedules projects and allocates resources, leading to fewer underfunded projects.

Stage 2 organizations make use of concurrent engineering. Because of the involvement of all the major functions from beginning to end of the project, strong incentive exists to do the job right from the beginning. Manufacturing has input in the early stages, and engineering does not abandon the project when it is time to scale it up. The use of dedicated teams and structured development process tends to encourage a high degree of parallelism and overlap between development activities.

Another advantage of the Stage 2 approach to product development is that some of the longer-horizon activities become much more meaningful. Product-line planning is now a cross-functional responsibility. Because product-line plans now influence the PAC and its decision making, and Core Teams in theirs, the process is much more valuable and given more serious attention. The distinction between individual projects and product lines is now more easily maintained. The Core Teams tend to develop individual projects in the context of product-line plans. The Product Approval Committee always has the option of combining separate projects or separating projects with overlarge scope into separate generations in response to a strategic product-line vision.

If Stage 1 companies tend to be internally focused when they set their targets, Stage 2 companies tend to focus much more externally. Targets for time and product performance tend to be based upon objective analysis of competitors and the use of benchmarking. The targets set in the early stages are fairly reliably met in the course of development.

Companies in Stage 2 often find themselves in the top 10–20% in terms of time to market and product quality. The time to market in Stage 2 is typically 40–60% of that in Stage 1. Clearly the move from Stage 1 to Stage 2 is one of the greatest improvements that a company can make. In highly competitive markets this is often a requirement for survival.

Stage 3—World-Class Product Development

Once companies have achieved integration of the functions in product development, they can continue to improve to be among the best in the world, the Stage 3 companies. These companies are typically marked by superiority in both domains: functional and technological excellence *and* excellence in their product development process.

In Stage 3 companies the development process, which is often quite similar to that in Stage 2, is now *fully ingrained and part of the culture.* New development projects are not seen as challenging the process, since the process is deeply imbedded in the culture. It is "how we do things."

Interestingly, as companies move from Stage 2 to Stage 3, and as this acculturation becomes more pronounced, certain aspects of this process may become less formal. As a practice becomes widely shared and understood, it requires less formal description or policing. Almost everyone in the organization effectively maintains the standard and keeps new people or those prone to go the wrong way using the major elements of the process in its true spirit.

In Stage 3, the existence of dedicated cross-functional teams such as Core Teams is now fully established. Colocation of team members is the rule; in fact colocation of major functions is quite common. The advantage in Stage 3 over Stage 2 is that development teams tend to be highly experienced. It is not unusual in Stage 3 companies for the same team to develop succeeding generations of the same product. The value of this long-term dedication is enormous. It produces learning-curve improvements and facilitates easy communication among team members. It also tends to keep projects from attempting too much. If the same team knows it will develop the next generation of product it will tend to stockpile good ideas for inclusion next time. These dedicated multiproject teams tend to have extremely short concept development times at the outset of projects. Such teams often begin developing the concept for the next generation of product concurrently with developing the actual current-generation product. As a result, capturing the next-generation concept on paper for an initial phase review often amounts to simply organizing the consensus of the team in an acceptable form.

Another characteristic of Stage 3 companies is their effective use of automation. They have a well-established integrated process that was achieved in Stage 2. Now they can automate steps in that process to achieve even greater improvements. They use many automated tools, including groupware for remote teams, CAD, and simulation models.

Improvements to the product development process are driven by an annual plan that identifies the best opportunities. Continuous improvement is measured, and these companies can achieve a 10–20% improvement in time to market each year.

World-class companies compare themselves to other world-class competitors as reference points for target setting. Targets are often stretch goals that other companies would consider impossible to achieve. (Note that these same goals, if set in earlier stages, would be unrealistic and counterproductive.) The assumption is that new product development can continually improve, and efforts are always under way to achieve those improvements. More often than not, these Stage 3 companies provide the benchmarks to which other competitors compare themselves.

One of the key indicators of Stage 3 status is that confidence in the product development process is so high that business strategies *explicitly* work to exploit this advantage. This exploitation may take several forms. In some cases, it will include attempts to overwhelm competitors through the rapid introduction of many new products. In other cases it takes the form of carefully timed new product launches to exploit trade shows or other events in the buying cycle. In industries with annual new product introduction cycles, for example, a development cycle shorter than 12 months offers enormous advantages. There is a built-in cushion for technical or competitive surprises. More time can be devoted up front on customer interactions to define product requirements. Increased reliability in terms of delivering on product announcements builds customer, distributor, and stock-market confidence, especially if competitors develop reputations for "vapor ware," or premature product announcements.

Stage 3 companies typically view the new product development process as a strategic advantage. This attitude naturally reinforces the time and effort they devote to maintaining this leading position. These companies have the best development cycle times in their industry and are usually gaining in market share as a result.

Progressing from Stage to Stage

In the context of new product development and the stages framework we are proposing, corporations are differentiated along two distinct dimensions, as shown in Figure 39.

One dimension relates to functional and technological excellence. Companies can be marked by various degrees of functional excellence or technical know-how. A second dimension is development-process capability. Independent of functional or technological excellence, this is skill in organizing, carrying out, maintaining, and improving complex business processes, such as new product development.

Companies that master one or the other tend to focus their thoughts and energies toward improving along that dimension. The technologically superior company tends to attract strong technical people and tends to reward achievement in innovation or in the generation of new patents, for example. The company focused on business process capability tends to reward people who make improvements to the business process.

A good way of assessing which dimension matters more is to think about the kinds of issues people typically devote a lot of their free time and energy to working on. When people go home after work, which problems are they most likely to be thinking about? Are the heroes in an organization functional or technological

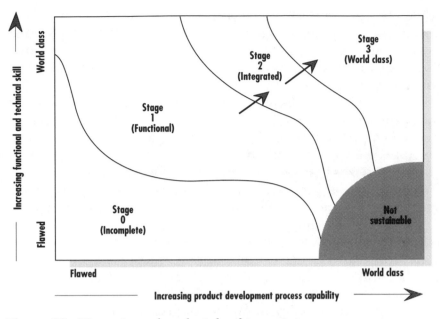

Figure 39. Dimensions of product-development stages.

heroes or business process heroes? Is the path toward general management along one or the other dimension?

With these two dimensions in mind, we can think about the evolution from stage to stage. The Stage 0 process can be marked by almost any degree of specific functional or technological skills; occasionally these skills can be quite high. On balance, however, at this stage business process capability is flawed. Start-ups that have at their core a technical superstar but lack necessary functions (such as manufacturing or an established product development process) exemplify this stage.

Stage 1 tends to favor functional and technological skill over business process excellence. Companies at this stage—which include the majority of companies—tend to have developed certain pockets of functional excellence, such as R&D, manufacturing, or sales. In this stage, the virtue of product development is that it respects the functional boundaries and the respective contributions of each function. It doesn't, however, get the most out of the blending of the functions. In short, Stage 1 companies may be world class in terms of their technical or functional input to the process but will only be average in terms of their business process capabilities. Sometimes these organizations trade off some functional strength for improvements in business process, but they come far short of being world class in the latter.

Stage 2 companies have successfully integrated all functions in their product development process. These companies have made a stepped improvement in their business process capability. The functions are well established but are also working together in a powerful process that gets the most out of that integration.

PACE typically involves taking companies from Stage 1 to Stage 2 and beyond. When companies move from Stage 1 to Stage 2, the functional and technological skills often are enhanced. When a well-integrated new-product development process exists, there is increased understanding of one function for the other, a clear identification of areas of recurring difficulty, and increased pull on the process for improved functional excellence.

Technology development provides a good example. As product development gets more integrated and cycle times come down, demand for technology development increases. The advantage of having technology on the shelf is markedly enhanced, and pull on the R&D organization tends to increase from the product development activity.

As companies achieve the benefits of integration, they see significant improvements in performance, but further improvements are still possible. World class development or Stage 3 product development is the stage marked by relative superiority in both business process and functional/technological skill. The companies in Stage 3 are among the world leaders and can be identified by their long-term record of new product development.

The rules of the game change constantly. Years ago most companies were functionally oriented. Today, the necessity of graduating to Stage 2 in order to be successful and competitive is widely understood, and the value of going to Stage 3 is self-evident.

Summary

Product development evolves through well-defined stages at all companies, and understanding this evolution helps a company see where it is and where it wants to go.

- In Stage 0 certain necessary elements of a product development process are either missing or extremely weak.
- Stage 1 is the classic stage during which product development responsibilities are distributed across strong functional organizations, and coordination takes place through hand-offs and internal contracts.
- Stage 2 is marked by functional integration at many levels, from the Core Team to the Product Approval Committee. It is the first true step toward product and cycle-time excellence.
- Stage 3 is achieved by the most successful product development organizations, is marked by a mix between functional (i.e., manufacturing) and business process (i.e., scheduling) excellence.
- PACE is a process for moving from Stages 0 and 1 to Stages 2 and 3.

11

Project Team Leadership

Why do some project teams quickly become fine-tuned synchronized units, enthusiastic and full of energy, while other project teams struggle to complete the simplest of tasks? The project leader is a key figure. There are many differences between project managers, who wield power and process information merely by routing people through their office, and true project leaders. Some of these differences are overt and obvious, while others are more subtle. Understanding the characteristics of good project leaders can be helpful to those with project responsibility, those who aspire to become project leaders, and those who are responsible for developing project leaders.

Working with the Project Team

Good project team leaders are scarce. In effective project teams such as Core Teams, they are true leaders—not managers, administrators, or clerks. Project leaders work with the team by

- understanding what is most critical for each person on the team
- motivating team members to achieve the best they can
- staying abreast of daily activities on the project
- building a team spirit that helps to form a consensus
- leading the team to resolve difficult issues
- freely and frequently communicating all project information to each team member
- shielding team members from non value-added activities

It is important for project leaders to have an understanding and basic knowledge of each team member's functional area. Project leaders must have cross-functional knowledge. They may not have intimate knowledge of each function, and many rely on project team members, but the leader must have a good understanding of the needs of each function and how it operates. Most importantly, a good leader asks the right questions.

Figure 40 shows the level of knowledge in each critical area for a project leader of a complex systems project. Note that the leader does not have to be the most technically expert person on the team. Rather, it is more important to be well rounded, with expertise or knowledge perspective *across* each function. By assessing a potential project leader's knowledge across these functional parameters, company managers can immediately understand the training required to get that person the skills necessary to excel.

By understanding what is important for each person on the team and what motivates each individual to excel, project leaders demonstrate their willingness to help people meet their goals through the project. For example, one software company had a highly efficient project leader assigned to spearhead the next release of its current product. She understood that the prior project glossed over testing and documentation, which made life extremely difficult for the testing and quality assurance

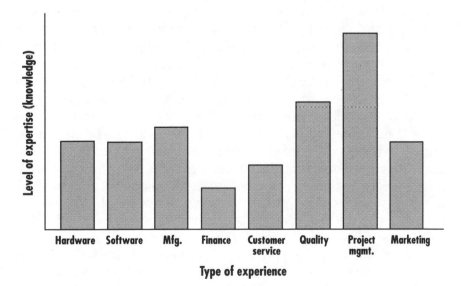

Figure 40. Knowledge and experience base for project leaders.

organizations. This also drove life cycle costs higher. People on her team from these organizations came to the meetings with preset agendas and attitudes. By taking the time to discuss their concerns and understand what was important to them, she won them over. Instead of dragging out every meeting with adversarial conflicts, the team truly jelled early into a cohesive unit. Time to market became a driving factor in their relationships.

In addition to feeling that their work is important to a winning project, team members must feel some sense of independence. Having a say over one's own activities and deadlines is critical to successfully motivating a project team. At minicomputer maker Data General, microcoders are frequently asked when they can get tasks completed. Many challenge themselves and put in place tighter deadlines than management had originally envisioned.

Motivation

Good project leaders also motivate each and every individual on the team to put in his or her absolute best effort. They have a knack for getting individuals to take actions that enable the team to get more done than the mere sum of individual efforts would suggest. This type of motivation comes from the leader's understanding of people. Good project leaders recognize first that individuals are, by necessity, self-centered. People like to think that they are part of a winning team working on a project that is critical to the company. Project leaders help people see the importance of their contribution and identify with winning.

For example, a bright young software engineer fresh out of school was working on modifying some existing code for a new networking product. The individual wasn't excited about this task because he perceived it to be trivial. By showing this person how critical that piece of code was, the project leader motivated the engineer to complete the task ahead of schedule. As a reward, this engineer was given more responsibility on the project and more challenging work. Good project leaders know that people are motivated by the same desire for praise and respect from peers that we all enjoy.

Motivation means to provide a motive, something that causes a person to take action. Motivation is generated by providing rewards when people accomplish key tasks. The good news is that often these rewards cost little. We have found that successful project leaders use the following reward mechanisms:

- Offering personal recognition that something has been completed. This can take place either one on one or in front of the entire team. Recognition also occurs when something has not been accomplished. It's important to provide positive feedback whenever possible but just as important to not let poor performance go unnoticed.
- Counseling members as to how they are doing, what they would like to do as a follow-on project, or what their individual training requirements are.
- Contributing awards that can be timed on a monthly or quarterly basis or for outstanding project performance. These awards can range from lunches, coffee mugs, pens, and plaques to cash awards and dinner certificates.
- Offering a chance to represent the project team either in house at a management review or project presentation or externally to customers or at trade shows.
- Ensuring that people have the right office equipment they need and an understanding that its use is flexible, for example, a phone call home each day should not be prohibited.
- Providing the proper tools to do the job right. This may entail scheduling equipment availability, purchasing a support contract, and involving the right people. The key things to watch for are inexpensive items that are wasting time.
- Creating project code names that serve as a flag to rally around. Even seemingly minor projects need a centerpoint.
- Improving the working environment, as in a little paint and some plants go a long way.
- Providing benchmarks as both a form of praise and as challenges to be overcome—to beat the competition.

Also effective is the recognition of motivational events or milestones in the project. One project leader actually schedules "planned randomness" into his own version of the overall project schedule. At critical milestones and important task completion points, he suddenly shows up with a minicelebration. It's usually something simple like donuts in the morning, Chinese food for lunch, or banners and balloons tied to the workstations. Corny? You bet, but it works. To the development project team, these events appear to occur on the spur of the moment. Each is carefully thought out and scheduled, however.

Creating friendly competition, if done in a positive light, can also do much to improve morale and increase productivity. One hardware engineering project team member from a consumer electronics company used to have "place and route" contests with the CAD group. He would place bets on who would finish a particular circuit board development first with the highest quality. The prize was a free lunch every day for a month. We've seen team members challenge each other on similar types of activities, where the loser has to wash each team member's car in the parking lot on a Friday afternoon. These types of light-spirited competitive events also go a long way toward alleviating the stress of getting the product out quickly. One of our clients sponsors a design challenge each year for all engineers. People have one week to make a self-propelled model racer out of nothing but popsicle sticks, rubber bands, and paper clips, for example. Developers look forward to these deviations from the grind, and although they may sound silly, productivity greatly increases immediately after these sorts of events.

Motivated individuals will sacrifice a great deal for companies that provide some meaning or sense of purpose to their work. In the early 1980s, for example, the minicomputer business was taking off, and the competitor with the latest system was sure to get a lot of press. Honeywell Information Systems motivated the development team to work day and night to support its project team's success in the market. The company provided cots and even installed a shower so that engineers working around the clock on system debug could be more comfortable.

Communication

A good project leader's worst enemies are a chair and desk. Instead of sitting in an office, a project leader should visit the project team members at least once a day, thus "managing by walking around." He or she must act as an information conduit, freely and frequently keeping team members informed of events and activities. At the same time, good project leaders are able to shield their team from distractions and people who are not actively contributing to the completion of the project.

Project leaders "have to be tenacious and want to make things happen," says Theresa Pratt, a core team leader of Codex Corporation, a division of Motorola.[1] They must be willing to "make noise at the top and ask embarrassing questions" when obstacles arise.

Traditional project managers expect people to come to them with problems to solve. They act more like dictators or bosses than team leaders. The leader serves as a quarterback who calls the plays (using an American football analogy), rather than a coach who runs the team. "I don't manage the project team, I lead them" says Sheila M. Mello, a BBN Communications Corporation Vice President and core team leader for a packet-switching product.[2] One minicomputer manufacturer had project managers who never left their offices except for "team beatings" that were based on the assumption that people worked harder if they were constantly harassed and threatened. This company's time to market never improved; in fact, it got longer, and the company was eventually bought out by a competitor.

Project leaders recognize that actions speak louder than words. People notice even small, seemingly insignificant actions of managers they deal with. As soon as words don't align with actions, a level of distrust develops that is often impossible to overcome. Project leaders are very careful about what they do and how it will be perceived by the development team.

Perhaps one of the most important roles of a project leader is responsibility to make sure that communication among team members happens on an ongoing basis. One microcomputer company's project leaders pride themselves on their ability to keep people talking to one another. To do this they facilitate easy and frequent face-to-face discussions. Colocating the project team, installing a coffee pot in the middle of the work area so people run into each other and discuss things over a cup, and having Friday afternoon pizza sessions are just some of the ways these project leaders keep this company's lines of communication open.

Problem Solving

Active involvement in problem solving is another role for successful project leaders. The discipline of seeing each problem through to complete resolution is embedded in good project leaders.

Throughout the development process, problems will surface

with project team members, between project team members, between project members and functional managers, and even with vendors and suppliers. The project leader is ultimately responsible for problem solving or the project will be delayed.

Working with Functional Managers

Successful project leaders understand that for long-term success they need to draw upon the strengths of functional mangers and not usurp their established place in the organization.

Poor project leaders attempt to isolate the functional manager to the point of not letting the function be involved in the project. The typical argument of these individuals is that by isolating their team from the rest of the company, the project will get done faster. Sometimes they are right, but this can also result in a design that is too costly, hard to manufacture, and difficult to service. Functional managers must be seen as the keepers of functional technical excellence. Project leaders then must draw upon this knowledge base for problem solving, issue resolution, and technical advice regarding the product's design and development.

Good project leaders begin to negotiate with functional managers up front about the project, resource requirements, timing, and trade-offs. The functional manager may be working with many project leaders. Resource planning and control will be a constant challenge for them. It is important for project leaders to be as flexible as possible yet still get their projects done properly and on time. This calls for close contact with the functional managers.

Throughout a project many issues arise. Some, like the competitive positioning of the product are significant. Others, like detail design alternatives are usually less significant. Issue escalation and resolution is another area where project leaders must draw on the support of the functional manager. Issues should be resolved at the lowest level possible since that is where the most accurate information lies.

On any major project, however, issues will arise that members of the project team can not resolve themselves. Resolution requires the project leader's involvement. The leader will have to work with the functional manager to resolve points of contention, resource availability, or other matters. If issues can not be resolved at this level, that's a failure for the project leader. Escalating issues to a level higher than the functional manager can result in a solution that is not beneficial to the project.

Finally, one of the most important interactions project leaders have with functional managers is reviewing technical aspects of the design—for that function's responsibility. For example, inviting the manager of software quality assurance to a code review, the functional head of hardware design to an architecture review, or the materials manager to a manufacturing process design review are excellent ways to bring years of technical knowledge in to review the product's design.

Working with Senior Management

Another important aspect of successful project leadership is the relationship with senior management. Formally this relationship exists through the Phase Review Process (see Chapter 3). Successful project leaders understand, however, that more frequent interaction is required with specific senior managers.

With responsibility for the overall direction of the company, senior management is very interested in product development. After all, products under development today will form tomorrow's revenue stream. There is literally nothing more important for senior management in any organization. Good project leaders must form a relationship with senior management to overcome difficulties they experience along the way.

Meeting one on one with senior management before a phase review is a good place to start. Project leaders should try to understand the concerns of each person and work those issues so that they can be properly addressed at the phase review. This not a pre-review of the upcoming phase review; it is taking the time to communicate in order to properly prepare the phase review.

What One Person Can Do

Let's suppose the project vision is clear to everyone; the team is right on track; everyone is psyched to work on the project. The hard work of planning is over, and the team's morale should run on its own, right? Wrong. Project leaders must, constantly, throughout the process provide recognition, motivational events, friendly competition, and the proper perspective.

In general, little things make the difference between mediocrity and excellence when leading a development project. It should come as no surprise if there is difficulty in getting people to work extra hours at a critical point in the project but the project leader is not there. To motivate a team to work harder for extended periods, two things are necessary. First, the team must see that there is a light at the end of the tunnel. People must know that if they get into this pattern to solve a temporary slippage that it does not condemn them to working 60 hours a week for the rest of their career with the company.

Second, if a team is expected to put in extra time, the leaders must also do so. To lead the way, the project leader must arrive at work *before* anyone else gets there. He or she must also stay until the very last person leaves. This must be done consistently every day until the project is back on track. It also doesn't hurt to come in on the weekend to help out or to do something to make the work place a little more enjoyable on Monday morning. Painting the walls, sweeping the floor and generally improving the appearance of the work environment are tasks well known to superior project leaders.

While being enthusiastic and positive are important, it is also critical not to become too predictable and thus ineffective. Various people, times, and situations demand different styles. Sometimes praise is needed, other times counseling is called for, other times reprimands are needed. There are times to be directive and times to listen. There are times to drive hard and times to ease off.

In conclusion, leadership takes place from the front and on the floor. It doesn't happen if you stay at your desk and expect things to naturally come to you. Superior project leaders must maintain constant contact with people and know what is happening around them.

Staying on top of the project, showing people that you are about it and that you fully expect it to make the schedule are critical to motivating people to work a little harder and a little longer in the interests of the project.

One final point: unless you believe in the project and that belief radiates from you (even when things aren't going well), there is no hope of leading a project team to excel. You cannot allow team members to see you discouraged or doubting. When the going gets rough, a good project leader we know takes a walk alone in the parking lot, calms down, and regains his composure before returning to the work area with a smile and a sense of renewed determination.

Summary

Aspiring to excellence in project leadership is a valuable objective for those involved in product development. Some of the ways of improving these skills include the following:

- Motivating the project team to a high level of performance.
- Facilitating communication so that the team operates smoothly.
- Taking the responsibility to solve problems and resolve issues
- Working effectively with functional managers.
- Earning the respect and confidence of senior management by effectively integrating them into the process.

References

1. Rick Whiting, "Core Team Leaders Call the Plays," *Electronic Business,* June 17, 1991, p. 54.
2. *Ibid.*

12

Implementing PACE: How to Make It Real and Make It Lasting

Prior to this chapter we have focused on the whys and whats of PACE—its benefits and its major processes. Having had a great deal of experience in implementing PACE, we will now share some of our insights into the hows of PACE—how to implement it and make it stick.

Because changing the way an organization develops products affects all functions and all levels of management, this entails major cultural change. Such change is difficult since people have operated for years in the present culture and many have achieved success in it. Now the rules of the game are changing and many will resist these alterations, even though the future viability of the company may be at stake.

Changing the rules is especially difficult because many rules are never made explicit. A company's culture is often largely invisible to those within it.

People don't become part of a company's culture right away. They go through rites of passage, and stumble, and learn to find their place in it over time. One day things that didn't make sense at first make perfect sense; in fact, they seem indispensable, inevitable. Experienced people share these insights with new people coming in who don't yet get it and are surprised at their apparent naïveté. New folks get it after a while, or they leave, but getting it and becoming part of it is hard work, and people don't change it easily.

We have helped many companies to implement PACE successfully and have encountered the impediments to success and overcome them. We have also studied how many companies have attempted to make fundamental improvements to product development only to find them ineffective or short-lived. The improvements never became truly institutionalized or ingrained in the culture. This is the goal of implementation: demonstrable, measurable, and widespread improvement that is self-sustaining and part of a *new culture* of continuous improvement.

The Implementation Experience: Mixed Reviews

A minicomputer company we visited is typical of many companies. After years of phenomenal growth it was facing a host of difficulties. Growth was slowing, at least in part because of protracted product development efforts. Products were announced but didn't ship. Although some competitors slipped too, others hit the market window in full stride and took significant market share. One of the delayed new products was introduced under pressure before the bugs had been ironed out. Service costs were extremely high as problems at the customer sites were addressed on the fly. There were so many changes to the design that the change order process was overwhelmed. Manufacturing ramp-up was delayed by all of this turmoil; which version were they ramping? Customers, many of them long-time loyalists, were complaining. One salesman confided to us that he was recommending that his customers not place orders; instead, he offered deep discounts on older generation equipment. Within the organization, morale was at a low ebb. Engineers on the troubled projects were living at the company, putting in 80 hours or more a week. Two highly regarded engineers, one in hardware and one in software, had recently left to join a smaller competitor, and rumors that resumes were on the street were common. "I'll tell you one thing for sure," one weary project manager told us, "I'll never go through this again."

Recognizing that something needed to be done, the vice president of engineering organized an internal task force. The team reviewed the current process, which was highly informal. Postmortems, as they were called, were held for several recently completed projects, detailing many specific problems and much dissatisfaction. It was decided that a new process was needed. A small team was assigned the task. It worked diligently and after several months produced a document describing the new development process, which was issued to the whole organization. This was done with much fanfare, including the distribution of laminated cards showing a high-level overview of the new process. Several project teams tried to use the process but for various reasons didn't follow through. Some were already too far along. Others encountered specific difficulties in following the document's recommendations. All found something to object to. One team felt it was too busy even to read it. The team that created the document met with many groups to encourage adoption. More often than not these meetings turned into gripe sessions. Gradually the authors lost interest and moved into positions that would subject them to less abuse. Six months after publication, not a single project was using the new process. Some people still had their laminated cards and used the high-level stage names to describe their project status, but the 3-inch vinyl notebook detailing the process was sitting on shelves, unopened and unused.

Why Implementation Is Difficult

Why is it so difficult for organizations to change? Why do so many companies make sincere efforts to improve product development without true success? There appear to be at least eight reasons why companies find this so difficult to achieve. Some of these relate to beliefs about what the change entails. Others relate to underestimation of the effort required or belief in piecemeal approaches or quick fixes. Some relate to the approaches used to implement these changes. Together they provide a good summary of the impediments to successful implementation.

1. *Awareness.* An absolute prerequisite for change is a common understanding of the current conditions, why they must change, and how specifically they must change. Since product development cuts across many functional areas, each with different problems and viewpoints, rarely is a common understanding of the underlying problems obvious. Rather there is a general feeling that one must do better along with sniping between functions. The realization that shared survival is at stake is buried.

Some companies have also investigated the best practices of

companies that are leaders in product development. This can provide proof that better methods exist, such as shorter cycle times, and more effective team structure. Rarely, however, do companies know how to tailor and implement these practices in their own organization based solely on these studies.

2. *Development not viewed as a process.* Another significant impediment is the lack of understanding that product development is a fundamental business process. Chapter 10 described the stages that companies go through as they improve this process. One basic premise is that at every stage a coherent process is in place, one with characteristic strengths and weaknesses. Many companies have not yet realized that this is one of the most important business processes that they manage. Without this realization they tend to focus their energies on improving the next development effort but not the overall development process. Recognizing that improving the development process is one of the most valuable initiatives a manager can undertake is vital to the success of the implementation.

3. *Who owns the problem?* Product development is, by its nature, cross-functional and involves many management layers. If development times are slow, whose problem is it? In a broad sense, it is everyone's problem, but that observation is too broad to be helpful. In most organizations the problems of product development are seen as belonging to some function or another, and the temptation is to expect that function to fix it on its own. This may be R&D in some organizations or engineering or marketing. In fact, it is highly unusual for one function to be able to effectively make the kinds of changes required for significant improvement. So many of the changes required are outside the control of any one person or group. The process whereby management decisions are made is especially difficult for all but the highest levels to address effectively. It is not unusual for a function, having been blamed for the development woes of an organization, to react defensively rather than constructively.

4. *Piecemeal approaches.* Throughout this book we've identified individual processes that must be addressed in some integrated fashion. Almost every chapter identifies specific improve-

ments that are of value in and of themselves. Unfortunately, the value they provide individually is a fraction of the value they provide when addressed in concert with the others. Many organizations latch onto one or another improvement and try to implement it without the related changes. For example, companies may design a new structured development process without addressing the issues of project organization or project review. Typically such processes end up on the shelf and not used. Other organizations focus on the structures of teams and form Core Teams or similar structures, without addressing the Phase Review Process or how scheduling is to take place. Such teams may be effective on one or two projects, but the improvements are hard to sustain throughout the entire portfolio of projects. In short, the only effective way to improve new product development is to improve all the elements and not attempt free standing and piecemeal improvements.

5.   *Underestimation of the effort required.* This is very common. Implementation of the improvements embodied in PACE is an effort that touches everyone in an organization. There are literally thousands of changes, some major and many minor, affecting most functions and levels of management. These changes must be implemented without disrupting day-to-day operations. Changes on this scale cannot occur without affecting power relationships, which may be fiercely defended. What will be rewarded usually changes too, and that alters the very contract that people make with their organization. The changes cannot help but challenge old beliefs and ideas. Successful implementation of PACE, defined as the full internalization of the process in the organization, takes several years. Results can be seen in a matter of months, and this helps the process along, but the full implementation requires that many people have gone through a new experience and learned how to make it part of what they do. This can only happen over time and on the basis of real and documented success. Managers whose horizons are too short may find it hard to champion such far-reaching change.

6.   *Changing management and management priorities.* Given the need to maintain steady support and pressure to successfully implement PACE, management's role is vital. If management changes

frequently as happens in some organizations, each new management team will tend to go at the problem anew. This uses up a great deal of goodwill in an organization. A fundamental improvement to a business process should be one that outlives any particular management team. Similarly, if management priorities change or too many initiatives are attempted at once, the organization tends to pay less serious attention to these initiatives, preferring to wait them out.

7. *The assumption that writing down a new process is enough.* This is very common. When many organizations attempt to improve product development, they may ask their people to create a new process. By this they often mean to document a new process. It is very difficult and perhaps impossible to change an organization simply by creating and documenting new procedures and publishing them. It is, unfortunately, much easier to create new documentation than it is to get people to read it and use it in its true spirit. Any documentation of a new process will be flawed. People will fasten on the flaws as reasons to reject the process. If there are no related changes in the organization that provide incentives to use the new process and disincentives for ignoring it, it is extremely unlikely that the new process will be used. We have rarely gone into an organization and found a complete lack of documentation of the product development process. It is more common to find that the process has been documented and "improved" many times, and that this documentation in its many generations rests in vinyl notebooks on shelves. The true test of implementation is whether the process is being used and used for all major development projects.

8. *The lack of continuous improvement structures.* Once an organization has gone through all the trouble of making fundamental improvements to the product development process, how will it sustain and maintain that process? How will it continue to learn from its experience with using the process? How will it capture those learnings in the process itself so that later projects benefit from the experiences of earlier ones? None of this happens automatically. There must be structures in place to help with continuous improvement. These structures include the identification of a process owner or a PACE engineer who will maintain and improve

the process. There must be periodic reviews of the process, based on well established metrics. There must be a central library of phase review documentation so that later projects can turn to them. There must be recurrent training and project facilitation. All of these activities require effort, and in companies that have successfully implemented PACE, these activities are highly valued and well supported. In a recent benchmark study we found that divisions with annual sales of between $300 million and $500 million were devoting approximately ten man-years every year to the maintenance of their product development process. This is the true cost of supporting continuous improvement. The benefits are that the process grows, improves, and does not atrophy.

Although these impediments are serious, they can be identified and overcome. In the next section, we'll talk about some of the key requirements for successful implementation.

The Keys to Successful PACE Implementation

There are six keys to successful PACE implementation; they are the ways to overcome the impediments we've just described. They overcome the inertia and skepticism in the organization. Every successful PACE implementation makes use of all of them.

1. *Getting ready.* An organization must be ready before it will change. Successful PACE implementations are preceded by activities that clarify and focus understanding of the need to improve the product development process for all functional areas and levels of management. Some companies are proactive and adopt a leading-edge process in anticipation of its benefits. Unfortunately in many companies it takes a crisis such as a revenue decline, a major product failure, or the loss of key people before the organization comes to the realization for the need to change.

A few senior managers at a fast growing company that designs and manufactures material tracking equipment recently attempted to begin the change process. Over the course of a three-day seminar with all of its technical management it delved into the causes of its chronic product introduction lateness, product redesigns, and project team coordination problems. Keeping focus on the problems related to the development process was difficult—it was more fun to talk about technical design approaches and the latest design tools. After the session the consensus of the group was to do nothing, although the warning signals were there that the product development process was not working. The managers had missed the opportunity to solve their problems early, before the crisis hit.

2. *Planning.* Since PACE is a complex process cutting across the entire organization, an explicit, detailed, and well understood implementation plan is critical. The first step is to determine the goals, or targets, of the implementation. These targets include timing of roll-out to all development programs, reduction in cycle-time, and performance to development program commitments such as schedule, budget, and success rate. These targets clearly identify what is at stake for the organization and the expected benefits.

The next step is to develop an actionable implementation plan with the correct actions, sequence, and responsibilities. One dilemma is that the implementor can easily identify more areas that need fixing than can possibly be tackled at once. The implementor is a bit like a triage nurse who deals with the life-threatening problems first and postpones other areas until later. Obviously, this plan must be well thought out and based on experience or the patient may die.

An equipment supplier to the cable TV industry completed an investigation into problems with its product development process. The division president, after hearing recommendations for improvement, latched onto the Core Team as the solution to his problems. Several of his vice presidents cautioned him that a plan was needed to carefully roll out all elements of PACE. After brushing aside their concerns, the president put a Core Team in charge of a group of important projects. Other, more important, problems with the development process were ignored. Soon the lone Core Team dissolved in frustration, with the organization becoming even more disillusioned than before.

3. *Role of management.* Successful implementation is not possible without the active support and appropriate participation of

all levels of management. Senior management, in particular, wants to be both a champion and a participant. Most managers underestimate their role in PACE implementation, which includes planning, project selection, resource allocation, and empowering teams.

A minicomputer company released a major new product after four years of frantic development. Trying to get the development team enthusiastic about the next project, senior management asked an internal manager to determine why it had taken so long and what it would take to fix the problem "down there," meaning with the engineers. In reality, most of the problem was management's continual changing of the project's direction and shifting of staff. After several months of effort, a new product development process was defined and implemented, primarily at the project team level. Initially management made the tough decisions required but then backed off and settled into its old habits. This company's development process improved marginally, but it missed the opportunity for dramatic improvement because of its management's reluctance to support and play its part in the new process.

4. *Building gradually*. In implementation it is crucial to build gradually and learn by doing. Organizations can only absorb so much change at once. Often when implementing PACE there is a lack of experience and skills in critical areas, especially in the role of Core Team leader. This brings to mind a quote of Robert Lovett's, an advisor to President Kennedy during the Cuban missile crisis. He said "Good judgment is usually the result of experience, and experience is frequently the result of bad judgment." In a PACE implementation, all experience—good and bad—is highly leveraged by application of learnings to other projects.

A consumer electronics company achieved substantial improvements in its early application of PACE concepts to a few projects. Delighted with the results, the president decided to roll out the process to all development projects concurrently. The result was chaos—teams weren't properly trained, cross-project management techniques were not yet in place, management was not capable of directing all the teams at once. Very quickly the initial gains in product development process improvements were lost.

5. *Providing help.* Many people in the organization will have to learn new roles and take on new responsibilities. Having experienced facilitators to help and encourage will greatly improve the transition to the new process. Training in various forms must also be provided to Core Teams, middle managers, and the PAC. We have found that traditional training practices, where the entire organization is trained at once (e.g., TQM training), are inappropriate. Instead, the ideal training philosophy is just in time, meaning training only those who will apply the new methods immediately before they begin their work.

A division of an international electronics company completely revamped its product development process. The process was rolled out first to a few and then to more projects. Since the roll-out was progressing smoothly, facilitation was deemed unnecessary. Soon the roll-out stagnated—the organization had not yet completed the transition to the new process. Facilitators were brought back to complete the roll-out.

6. *Continuous improvement.* Continuous improvement is the path to world class performance. For continuous improvement to occur, everyone in the organization has to be involved and a specific group designated with its primary purpose to continue to improve the process and combat the tendency toward complacency.

A data communications company, after fully implementing an improved product development process, formed a PACE group headed by a director-level individual. This group facilitates development projects, conducts ongoing training, works with functional managers to improve cycle time in their areas, benchmarks other leading companies to learn new methods, and continues to identify additional opportunities for improvement. After the initial dramatic improvement, this company's product development cycle time continues to decrease 15–20% per year.

Applying PACE to Multiple Industries

While there are many similarities in product development processes across companies, there are obviously differences as well. PACE, as a process for product development, needs to be modified to fit the specific needs of different industries and companies. We have had extensive experience in modifying PACE. The following are several examples.

1. *Semiconductor devices and process industries.* In semiconductor devices and process industries, process development is often more important and time consuming than product or device design. For semiconductors, for example, development of the fabrication process requires intensive effort. This may necessitate a separate process development structure. In some development projects the process development will be done first. Only when development is far enough along will phase reviews of products begin.

2. *Complex mechanical equipment.* Complex products with multiple mechanical subassemblies frequently need to distinguish the development of the new subassemblies from the final product. In some cases it is better to decouple the subassembly development from the final system if the subassembly module is totally new and applicable to multiple products. This decoupling must be overcome by other integrating mechanisms such as overlapping Core Teams.

3. *Computer software.* Computer software products rely significantly on the structure of the development process and the effectiveness of the Core Teams to speed development. The development structure needs to be a little deeper in the software activities and the Core Team needs to be broadened a little. The use of such techniques as structured software design and automated tools can have a big payback.

4. *Consumer products.* The seasonality and short life cycles for consumer products affects both the Phase Review Process and the steps in the process. They both need to be related directly to the customer purchasing cycle and the timing of industry trade shows. For example, the development schedule for a seasonal product should start immediately after the early results for that season in one year and be completed in time for the next. This puts emphasis on close integration of product strategy with the development process.

5. *Compliance-based industries.* In several industries the need for compliance with government requirements influenced product development throughout. In sectors of aerospace and defense compliance with government or customer contracting requirements dominate. The challenge is to recognize these requirements and comply with them efficiently. Actions to maximize the reimbursability of development done for the government are not always consistent with best development practices. The appropriate development structure can help by recognizing contracting as a key development function and focusing on ways of being compliant yet efficient.

6. *Medical products.* Companies developing medical products have to comply with unique requirements for clinical testing and government approvals before release of their products. This may take months or even years to complete, but the appropriately structured development process can reduce this time by eliminating unnecessary delays. Additionally, executive officers of medical products companies may be directly liable for deficiencies in testing and release. This places even more importance on an effective Phase Review Process.

7. *Biotechnology industries.* Biotechnology products have a particularly long development cycle since they typically have government approval requirements and require lengthy research cycles. The transition from research to development can be greatly improved with the right structure and an effective Phase Review Process.

8. *Advanced materials and parts.* These are often highly science-based industries with a high degree of basic research. Integrating research and development explicitly in the process is critical. Understanding the customers is also highly critical, especially recognizing the true value of the product to the customer. The true value of a part may be unrelated to the cost of manufacturing it. PACE is modified in these industries to highlight these issues, linking research to in-depth understanding of the customer.

9. *International operations.* Development is increasingly an international activity, with related activities in different locations

and continents. Increasingly developers are asked to address global markets and accommodate local differences in requirements and standards. In these cases PACE is modified to effectively integrate and harmonize development practices across sites. A unified development process with a global PAC and blended Core Teams support this goal.

10. *Telecommunications.* The many international requirements that have to be considered for telecommunication equipment companies make them prime candidates for PACE. The development process must include internationalization issues and DFE principals. In addition, user-oriented design is directly related to how well products sell in international markets.

11. *Components.* Sorting out the diversity of product lines to leverage core competencies is a key consideration for component manufacturers. Most component companies have more ideas for new products coming in each month than they can evaluate. The structured process and Phase Review elements of PACE are vital to properly managing these challenges.

Leading the Change in the Product Development Process

Successful implementation of an improved product development process involves the efforts of many people. Understanding these roles helps to provide an understanding of how implementation should be approached.

The Role of the Outsider

We have been describing an implementation approach derived through practice and experience. It is steady and reliable if the pitfalls can be avoided. It requires a clear vision of how successful implementation is achieved, wedded to a practical ability to make mid-course corrections and adjust the process.

Implementation can succeed without an outsider such as an implementation consultant, but a good implementation consultant can make success sure, less painful, and occur more quickly. The outsider brings experience, which is invaluable. He or she brings a clearer vision of what must be accomplished first and what may be deferred. He or she may bring some objectivity and a distance from internal, political issues. In particular, the experienced PACE implementor will be more likely to succeed in those activities focused on senior management than a member of that management's organization. There is a trade-off to be made. Internal staff can succeed in a PACE implementation, but they must be among the very best leaders and managers and they must be given unusual freedom to operate across the organization. There is an opportunity cost associated with putting such people on the job, one many companies find difficult to justify. There is also the issue of time. An assisted PACE implementation can generally proceed faster than an unassisted one. Our experience has shown that an adequately planned for and resourced implementation assignment always leads to significant and measurable improvement.

The Role of Middle Management

Middle managers from all functions, senior individual contributors, technical specialists, and technical managers all play a significant role in changing the product development process. They have the prime responsibility to define and implement the details of the new process.

Their role begins with defining the changes necessary to the current product development process. This requires understanding the current process as well as the specific opportunities for improvement. The changes need to make sense as both part of an overall architecture and individually. This initially involves defining an overall decision-making process such as a Phase Review Process, establishing an effective approach to project-team organization like the Core Team approach, and clearly structuring the detailed activities of product development. Following that, the other elements of the overall product development process—product strategy, technology management, design techniques and development tools, and cross-project management—need to be upgraded.

They also need to guide the implementation of the changes. This is particularly challenging because process changes such as this are cross-functional and involve the cooperative effort of those with different objectives. This requires managers from all functional areas to make compromises for the greater good of the company as a whole.

In our experience in implementing improvements to the product development process, this is where the best middle managers stand out. They rise above the others to lead the change, putting in the extra effort and making the personal sacrifices necessary. Changing a process as complex and involved as product development is not easy, and only the best will be able to do it.

The Role of the CEO

A company's CEO or general manager has the primary responsibility for improving its product development process, and in many cases it is the most important contribution that the CEO can make to the long-term success of the company. New products drive the growth and prosperity of most companies. Yet, a CEO can't lead every product development activity—there is not enough time available, and usually the CEO does not have the technical skills. The CEO can, however, lead the creation of the best possible process for developing new products.

The CEO can initiate the change process. This entails setting new objectives for product development, establishing a new direction for the process of developing products, and launching the project to change that process. This provides the vision necessary for everyone in the company to make these very difficult changes.

Unfortunately the CEO could also provide a faulty vision that may eventually lead to the company's demise. Through inaction, the CEO automatically conveys that the status quo is acceptable. Competitors can take advantage of this complacency to achieve significant advantage. Worse yet, the CEO could provide the wrong vision. At one company, for example, the CEO acted forcefully to change product development by issuing an edict that everyone had to work ten-hour days, seven-days a week, including holidays, in order to develop more new products. If they didn't, they were automatically fired. The best developers thought this was childish and immediately resigned. Product development quickly deteriorated.

In our experience in implementing improvements in product development, the CEO's leadership is most essential when the change process is at that difficult juncture when the new process is partially, but not yet fully, implemented. The benefits are not yet apparent—but the stress of the change on individuals is. Some see their responsibilities changing and are uncertain what they will be doing when things change; so they question the changes that impact them. In successful implementations, this is where the CEO steps in and supports the change by communicating confidence that the company is going in the right direction.

The product development process will be the battleground of the 1990s; a battle that will change the competitive balance of some industries. Companies with a superior process can increase revenue more rapidly, maintain higher development productivity, and achieve operational efficiencies. When achieved simultaneously these benefits establish a significant competitive advantage.

Over the long term, the only sustainable source of product advantage for a company is to have a product development process that is superior to that of its competitors. The CEO has the responsibility to lead the company to that advantage—to win the battle of the 1990s.

Glossary

Consistent definitions of the elements of product development do not yet exist and many new terms are defined for the first time in this book. This glossary of terms is provided to clarify terminology used in this book. Definitions are cross referenced to each other by italics in the definition.

activities Within a *structured development* process, activities at the level below *tasks*.

automated design/development tools Tools that automate or improve development tasks, such as computer aided design (CAD).

concurrent engineering An approach to new product development where the product and all its associated processes, such as manufacturing, distribution, and service, are developed in parallel. Typically this involves *cross-functional* involvement early in the project. Also known as simultaneous engineering.

Core Team An effective approach to project team organization developed by PRTM in the mid-1980s. A core team is a small cross-functional team—typically depicted as a wheel structure—empowered to develop a new product.

Core Team leader The manager of the Core Team, with the overall leadership responsibility for leading the project; more a leader than a superior.

core technologies The primary technologies that support a company's new *product strategy*.

cross-functional The involvement of multiple functions working on common development *steps* at the same time instead of sequentially.

cross-project management The management of those activities such as *resource allocation* and *portfolio management* that affect multiple projects. This is also an element of the *PACE* process.

cycle time The time required to complete a particular process, such as the *product development process*.

cycle-time guidelines Within PACE, a characterization of a company's product development process at the *step* level from a time perspective that is used for scheduling and continuous improvement; a standard costing for time.

design for excellence (DFE) Design approaches that incorporate more than performance or features into product design. Includes such techniques as design for manufacturability, design for assembly, design for testability, design for serviceability, and design for green (environmental considerations).

design techniques Practices used in new product development to design products better and faster. Each technique has a specific focus.

detailed development guidelines A set of procedures and aids for accomplishing development *steps*. These are the how to of the process.

empowerment The act of giving a group, typically a project team, the responsibility and authority to do a specific job. Should not be confused with letting them do anything they want without an approval process.

engineering change orders (ECOs) The documentation and process for changing products once they are released.

full project team The full team involved in development, including the *Core Team* and the *support team*, those outside of the *Core Team,* many of whom are not dedicated to one project.

future core technologies The core technologies of the future, with the potential to alter the rules of the game.

new product-line innovation The element of *product strategy* that focuses on opportunities for new product lines.

PACE (Product And Cycle-time Excellence) A term introduced by *PRTM* that defines both a philosophy (achieving excellence in the quality and success of new products while simultaneously achieving the shortest time to market) and an approach to implementing the philosophy; a framework that integrates the elements of the *product development process.*

PACE engineer The *PACE* process owner after implementation; responsible for continuous improvement and *product development process engineering.*

phase A major stage of product development within a *Phase Review Process.* Each phase has specific requirements that projects must fulfill to continue into the next phase.

phase review The milestone at the end of a *phase* in a *Phase Review Process* where approval is required in order to proceed. Usually this requires resolving specific questions.

Phase Review Process The process within *PACE* where senior management (as a *PAC*) approves new product development, allocates development resources, and prioritizes activities. Within PACE, this is an action-oriented process that implements *product strategy* and initiates *empowerment* of *Core Teams*. It does so through a series of focused and efficient meetings.

portfolio management The process for managing the types of projects in order to achieve a strategic mix of technologies, timeframe, risk, markets, and business segments.

Product Approval Committee (PAC) The senior management group that has the authority and responsibility to approve and prioritize new product development within a *Phase Review Process*. Sometimes called by other terms such as product review board, executive committee, strategy committee.

product development process The overall business process for developing new products. While frequently referred to, there is no generally accepted description of how it actually works.

product development process engineering The responsibility for planning and continuous improvement of the product development process itself. A responsibility of the *PACE engineer*.

product-line expansion The element of *product strategy* that focuses on expanding current product lines.

product-line mapping A time-phased view of a product line's evolution.

product positioning A *product strategy* technique for defining products to have strategically favorable advantages in the market relative to competitors.

product strategy The process for linking a company's business strategy to product development by providing a vision for product development and competitive positioning of new products. Also used to describe an element in the *PACE* process.

project overview Within *structured development*, this is a one-page vision of the entire project at the *phase* and *step* level.

project team organization How people developing a new product work together, typically including the definition of responsibilities and authorities.

PRTM Pittiglio Rabin Todd & McGrath

resource scheduling The allocation and prioritization of resources, primarily people, assigned to development projects.

quality function deployment (QFD) A disciplined approach to planning, communicating, evaluating, and documenting customer requirements and then translating them into design activities.

simplified quality function deployment (S-QFD) An efficient variation of *quality function deployment* developed by *PRTM* for complex products.

step The level below *phase* within *structured development;* steps consist of multiple *tasks* and are used to schedule and manage the progress of development.

structured development A hierarchically based blueprint for product development that successively defines development at several levels. It is also used to describe an element within the *PACE* process.

support team Those active in a development project but not on the *Core Team;* the outer ring in a Core Team chart.

task The level below *steps* within *structured development;* tasks define in more detail how a step is done and consist of a number of *activities*.

technology management The element of the PACE *product development process* that identifies new technologies, determines *core* and *future core technologies,* and initiates technology-development projects.

technology unbundling A technique of *technology management* used to identify core technologies.

three-level scheduling A scheduling technique based on *structured development*.

time to market The product development *cycle time* from initial product concept to stable manufacturing.

Index